❖ MARY FORD ❖
MAKING
CAKES
— FOR —
MONEY

Contents

Author

Mary Ford has been teaching the art of cake-making and decorating for three decades. Working with her husband, Michael, she has produced over twenty step-by-step books demonstrating the various skills and techniques of the craft. Her books have gained a worldwide reputation for expertise and imagination combined with common sense and practical teaching ability. Her unique step-by-step approach with the emphasis on self-explanatory colour illustrations is ideally suited for both beginners and enthusiasts.

Preface

This book is intended for the amateur cake maker and decorator working from their own kitchen and producing cakes for stalls at fêtes, charity occasions and the like. It is also intended for the amateur producing cakes for friends and neighbours' parties and special occasions. If you intend to start a business in this area you are strongly recommended to consult an accountant or other professional adviser.

As a hobbyist cake decorator you should be aware:

i) the costing system is dependent on the accuracy of your calculation of the ingredients used, and the "overhead" and "profit" calculation explained on pages 6 to 10.

ii) the Food Hygiene and other legislation may be relevant to you. You should be aware, if you are selling to "the public" of the need to satisfy current legislation on such matters as weights & measures, product description and contents labelling.

This book does not address these issues and if in doubt, you are advised to consult an industry specialist or the appropriate government body for advice and guidance.

This edition published in 1999 by
Mary Ford Books a division of Michael O'Mara Holdings,
9 Lion Yard, Tremadoc Road, London SW4 7NQ
© 1999 Mary Ford Books a division of Michael O'Mara Holdings.

First published 1989
Revised edition published 1994
© Mary Ford Publications Ltd & Mary Ford Books Ltd.

Made and printed in China

ISBN 1–85479–421–3

1 3 5 7 9 10 8 6 4 2

Introduction

This Mary Ford reference book accurately and concisely trains everyone who wants to make his or her hobby pay for itself to price the making, baking, coating and decorating of any one of the twenty-two original Mary Ford cake designs featured on pages 29–113 (or, indeed, any other cake the enthusiast wishes to produce).

Easy-to-use COST SHEETS, COST SUMMARY FORMS and ORDER FORMS are depicted (with blank Master Copies on pages 114–117, which can be copied and used for updating records when, for example, ingredient or product costs rise). Each recipe and cake design is fully supported – in the Mary Ford tradition – with step-by-step pictorial and written instructions.

Work notes and timings *are actually recorded in the book by the cake decorator* – to become a permanent record – and, likewise, the COST SUMMARY assigned to each cake design is completed by the cake decorator from the working COST SHEETS. It will be seen that each stage of the work on a cake is separately costed on its own COST SHEET.

Cake decorators, who regularly make cakes for sale, can photograph each finished cake and display it in a special album with its details and sale price. (It should, perhaps, be noted that, to meet customer demands, alternative prices could be featured – reflecting the different costs between, say, a light fruit cake and a sponge cake, or the use of artificial flowers instead of sugar flowers.)

No longer need the cake icing enthusiast worry about "what to charge" the friend, relative or neighbour for producing that superb celebration cake.

Mary Ford has, yet again, come to the rescue!

HOW THE SYSTEM WORKS

The first step is to calculate the cost of the cake base using the 'CAKE COST SHEET'.

The second step is to cost the covering and coating to be applied to the cake.

The third step is to carry forward the cost of the cake base and the proportionate cost of the covering and coating used, to the 'COATED CAKE COST SHEET'.

Finally in the fourth step a 'COST SUMMARY FORM' is produced setting out the total cost of the decorated cake. This form can be retained as a working record for use when quoting prices to a purchaser.

Mary Ford has selected Wayne, the light fruit cake described in detail on pages 81–84, to illustrate the costing system. A full explanation in step-by-step format of the method of costing is on pages 6–10.

STEP 1

Costing the Cake

The CAKE COST SHEET opposite shows the ingredients used and time spent on preparing and making the cake base for Wayne. After the ingredients have been weighed and costed, subtotal 'A' is calculated. This comes to £3.00.

The HEAT used for baking the cake is difficult to calculate accurately and may be estimated by multiplying the total ingredients cost by 10%. This gives a figure of 30p.

It is essential to maintain a list of other items used which should be recorded under the heading 'Products'.

To cost properly the time taken to make and decorate any cake, it is necessary to –

A Record the time taken to complete each area of work (to enable this to be done, every working page of the book allows notes and times to be logged); and

B Choose a realistic and marketable labour charge which reflects accurately the skills, techniques and experience involved. (For her sample work on the cake Wayne, Mary Ford chose an hourly rate of £3.00, which converts to 5 pence per minute.)

In preparing and making the cake base for Wayne 60 minutes was taken, giving a labour charge of £3.00 (subtotal 'D').

TABLE		
CHARGE PER HOUR		CHARGE PER MINUTE
60p	=	1p
£1.20	=	2p
£1.80	=	3p
£2.40	=	4p
£3.00	=	5p
£3.60	=	6p
£4.20	=	7p
£4.80	=	8p
£5.40	=	9p
£6.00	=	10p

Finally, the subtotals 'A', 'B', 'C' and 'D' are totalled to give a cost of £6.50.

This cost gives an accurate value for the cake base and will be used for calculating the coated cake on the 'COATED CAKE COST SHEET' on page 9.

With a variety of ready made cakes available on the market, the decorator may wish to purchase a light fruit cake. In which case the purchase price should be used on the Coated Cake Cost Sheet.

Blank 'MASTER' COST SHEETS are on pages 114–116.

CAKE COST SHEET

CAKE __Light Fruit__   NAME __Wayne__   BOOK __M.C.F.M.__   PAGES __81–84__

DATE MADE __25th February__   SIZE __20.5cm (8in)__   SHAPE __Square__

A INGREDIENTS	Weight	Cost
Butter	225g (8oz)	56p
Caster Sugar	225g (8oz)	16p
Ground Almonds	60g (2oz)	25p
Fresh Egg	225g (8oz)	28p
Self Raising Flour	225g (8oz)	10p
Cherries (halved)	170g (6oz)	54p
Cherries (chopped)	60g (2oz)	18p
Currants	170g (6oz)	20p
Sultanas	225g (8oz)	26p
Mixed Peel	115g (4oz)	14p
Rum	30g (1oz)	23p
Lemon Zest & Juice	1	10p
	Subtotal A = £	3.00

C PRODUCTS	Used	Cost
Greaseproof Paper	½ sheet	3p
White Fat	45g (1½oz)	2p
Waxed Paper	1 sheet	15p
	Subtotal C = £	20p

D TIME TAKEN	Minutes
Weighing	16
Preparing Tin	6
Making The Cake	38
Total	60
Charge per minute	× 5 p
Total	3.00
LABOUR CHARGE Subtotal D = £	3.00

B HEAT
10% of ingredients' cost   Subtotal B = £ __30p__

Subtotals A + B + C + D =

TOTAL COST = £ __6.50__

(Carry forward to
COATED CAKE COST SHEET)

Blank 'MASTER' COST SHEETS are on pages 114–116.

STEP 2

Costing Coverings and Coatings

To calculate the cost of the covering and coating of any cake it is necessary to record the ingredients used and the time taken in preparing and making them.

The Cost Sheets below show the total cost for producing a specific amount of almond paste and royal icing. They show the total cost for 905g (2 lbs) of almond paste came to £3.20 and a similar amount of royal icing to £1.50.

Every cake in the book is accompanied by profile information which gives the approximate ingredients and materials required to complete the cake. The profile for Wayne is on page 81.

Once the cake has been covered and coated the actual amount of almond paste and royal icing used must be calculated and charged accordingly. The amounts are then entered on the 'COATED CAKE COST SHEET' on page 9.

ALMOND PASTE COST SHEET		
DATE MADE 12th March		
A INGREDIENTS	Weight	Cost
Caster Sugar	170g (6oz)	12p
Icing Sugar (sieved)	170g (6oz)	18p
Ground Almonds	340g (12oz)	1.50p
Glucose Syrup	225g (8oz)	90p
	Subtotal **A** = £	2.70
B TIME TAKEN	Minutes	
Making	10	
Total	10	
Charge per minute	× 5 p	
Total	50	
LABOUR CHARGE Subtotal **B** = £		0.50
Subtotals **A** + **B** = TOTAL COST = £		3.20
TOTAL WEIGHT 905g (2lb)		

ROYAL ICING COST SHEET		
DATE MADE 19th March		
A INGREDIENTS	Weight	Cost
Pure Albumen Powder	22g (¾oz)	42p
Water	145g (5oz)	
Icing Sugar (sieved)	740g (26oz)	68p
	Subtotal **A** = £	1.10
B TIME TAKEN	Minutes	
Making	8	
Total	8	
Charge per minute	× 5 p	
Total	40	
LABOUR CHARGE Subtotal **B** = £		0.40
Subtotals **A** + **B** = TOTAL COST = £		1.50
TOTAL WEIGHT (approx) 905g (2lb)		

How to make ALMOND PASTE – pages 17–18

How to make ROYAL ICING – pages 19–20

Blank 'MASTER' COST SHEETS are on pages 114–116.

STEP 3

Costing the Coated Cake

The 'COATED CAKE COST SHEET' brings together the cost of the cake base (from the Cake Cost Sheet on page 7) and the covering and coating used (from the information on page 8). Consequently it will be seen that the £6.50 representing the cake base cost is the first item on the products list. The other products used are then entered to achieve a total product cost.

Once again it is very important to record and charge the time taken in covering and coating the cake. Mary Ford took 26 minutes which was charged at 5p per minute giving a labour charge of £1.30 (subtotal 'B').

The subtotals 'A' and 'B' are then added together to give a total cost of £13.40 for the undecorated cake. This Cost is now carried forward to the 'COST SUMMARY SHEET' on page 10.

COATED CAKE COST SHEET

DATE	20th March	NAME	Wayne	BOOK	M.C.F.M.
PAGE	81	SIZE	20.5cm (8in)	SHAPE	Square
CAKE	Light Fruit	COVERING	Almond Paste	COATING	Royal Icing

A PRODUCTS	Used	Cost		B TIME TAKEN	Minutes
Light Fruit Cake	20.5cm (8in)	6.50p		Covering with A.P.	9
Cake Board	28cm (11in)	79p		1st Coat Top	3
Almond Paste	905g (2lb)	3.20p		1st Coat Sides	3
Apricot Purée	60g (2oz)	8p		2nd Coat Top & Sides	4
Royal Icing	680g (24oz)	1.12p		3rd Coat Top & Sides	4
Glycerine	30g (1oz)	36p		Coating Board	3
Colour	5 drops	5p			
				Total	26
				Charge per minute	× 5 p
				Total	1.30
				LABOUR CHARGE Subtotal B = £	1.30
		Subtotal A = £ 12.10		Subtotals A + B = TOTAL COST = £	13.40

Blank 'MASTER' COST SHEETS are on pages 114–116.

STEP 4

Costing the Decorated Cake

The final form is the 'COST SUMMARY SHEET'. This sheet includes £13.40 for the cost of the coated cake plus the other costs incurred, giving a total of £16.00.

COST SUMMARY – WAYNE

DATE __25th March__	NAME __Wayne__	BOOK __M.C.F.M.__
PAGE __81__	SIZE __20.5cm (8in)__	SHAPE __Square__
CAKE __Light Fruit__	COVERING __Almond Paste__	COATING __Royal Icing__

A PRODUCTS	Used	Cost	B TIME TAKEN	Minutes
Coated Cake	20.5cm(8in)	13.40p	Decorating	36
Royal Icing	170g (6oz)	28p		
Piping Bags	Greasepr'f	6p		
Keys	2	16p		
Horseshoe	1	11p		
Leaves	4	10p		
Board Ribbon	1½ metres	9p		
			Total	36
			Charge per minute	× 5 p
			Total	1.80
			LABOUR CHARGE Subtotal **B** = £	1.80
		Subtotal: **A** = £ 14.20		

Subtotals **A** + **B** = TOTAL COST = £ 16.00
*OVERHEAD COSTS = £ 0.80
*PROFIT COSTS = £ 1.60
***GRAND TOTAL** = £ 18.40

(* = See below)

OVERHEAD COSTS

'OVERHEAD COSTS' are the 'hidden' costs which do not appear on any of the 'COST SHEETS' (e.g. equipment, tool replacement, electric lighting, etc). One way of calculating the overhead cost is by adding a percentage rate – say 5% of the 'TOTAL COST' (£16.00) giving an overhead cost of £0.80p.

PROFIT COSTS

If a profit element is needed, it can be allotted at a fixed percentage rate – say 10% of the 'TOTAL COST' (£16.00) giving a profit cost of £1.60 therefore:

WAYNE'S TOTAL	£16.00
(plus) OVERHEAD COSTS	£ 0.80
(plus) PROFIT COSTS	£ 1.60
GRAND TOTAL =	£18.40

ORDER FORM

If the cake is to be supplied to a customer, it may be necessary to prepare an Order Form setting out details of the cake. A completed specimen order form is set out on page 117.

Note: A blank 'Master' COST SUMMARY is on page 116.

Genoese Sponge

WORK NOTES

PREPARING A SPONGE TIN
STEPS 1–3

TIME

STARTED _____

FINISHED _____

TIME TAKEN _____

MAKING
GENOESE SPONGE
STEPS 4–11

TIME

STARTED _____

FINISHED _____

TIME TAKEN _____

(Do not include the baking
time)

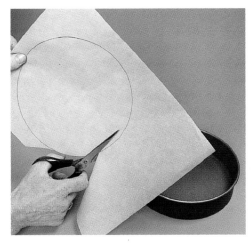

PREPARING A SPONGE TIN

1. Draw a circle on greaseproof paper, using a sponge tin as guide. Cut along the line to form a disc.

MAKING GENOESE SPONGE

4. Weigh all the ingredients, using the recipe on page 13. Place the butter and margarine in a mixing bowl. Beat until light.

2. Grease inside of tin with white fat, using a pastry brush.

5. Beat in the caster sugar.

3. Position disc in the tin, then grease the disc with white fat.

6. Lightly mix the eggs together. Then thoroughly beat in a small portion of egg at a time, until all egg is used.

WORK NOTES

7. Scrape down mixture from inside of bowl and then add the flour.

10. Spread mixture evenly with a spatula. Bake in centre of oven (180°C/350°F or Gas Mark 4).

8. Using a spatula, gently fold in the flour. Do not over-mix.

11. After baking, leave sponge in tin for 5 minutes, then turn out on to greaseproof paper sprinkled with caster sugar. Invert the sponge on to a wire tray and leave until cold.

STORAGE

Wrap the sponge in waxed paper and store in deep freeze for up to 6 months, or use within 3 days of making.

9. Place mixture in prepared tin.

Ingredients

(USING APPROPRIATE SIZE TIN).

TIN SIZE	18cm (7in) SQUARE OR 20.5cm (8in) ROUND		20.5cm (8in) SQUARE OR 23cm (9in) ROUND		23cm (9in) SQUARE OR 25.5cm (10in) ROUND		25.5cm (10in) SQUARE OR 28cm (11in) ROUND		28cm (11in) SQUARE OR 30.5cm (12in) ROUND	
BUTTER	45g	1½oz	65g	2¼oz	85g	3oz	115g	4oz	130g	4½oz
MARGARINE	45g	1½oz	65g	2¼oz	85g	3oz	115g	4oz	130g	4½oz
CASTER SUGAR	85g	3oz	130g	4½oz	170g	6oz	225g	8oz	255g	9oz
FRESH EGG	85g	3oz	130g	4½oz	170g	6oz	225g	8oz	255g	9oz
SELF RAISING FLOUR	85g	3oz	130g	4½oz	170g	6oz	225g	8oz	255g	9oz

BAKING TIMES	22 mins	23 mins	24 mins	25 mins	26 mins

Baking temperature 180°C/350°F or Gas Mark 4

CAKE COST SHEET

CAKE _____Genoese_____   NAME _____   BOOK _____   PAGE _____
DATE MADE _____   SIZE _____   SHAPE _____

A INGREDIENTS	Weight	Cost
Butter	____	____
Margarine	____	____
Caster Sugar	____	____
Fresh Egg	____	____
Self Raising Flour	____	____

Subtotal **A** = £ _____

B HEAT
10% of ingredients' cost   Subtotal **B** = £ _____

C PRODUCTS	Used	Cost
Greaseproof Paper	____	____
White Fat	____	____
Waxed Paper	____	____

Subtotal **C** = £ _____

D TIME TAKEN	Minutes
Preparing Tin	____
Making The Cake	____

Total _____
Charge per minute   ×   p
Total _____
LABOUR CHARGE   Subtotal **D** = £ _____

Subtotals **A** + **B** + **C** + **D** =
TOTAL COST = £ _____

NOTE: Please refer to the information on pages 5–7 before attempting to complete this COST SHEET.
A 'MASTER' Cost Sheet can be found on page 115.

Light Fruit Cake

PREPARING INGREDIENTS
STEP 1

TIME

STARTED   _____

FINISHED   _____

TIME TAKEN   _____

PREPARING CAKE TIN(S)
STEP 2

TIME

STARTED   _____

FINISHED   _____

TIME TAKEN   _____

MAKING THE CAKE
STEPS 3–6

TIME

STARTED   _____

FINISHED   _____

TIME TAKEN   _____

(Do not include the baking
time)

PREPARING INGREDIENTS

1. Weigh and prepare all the ingredients, using the recipe on page 16. Leave in a warm place (18°C/65°F) for 12 hours.

PREPARING CAKE TIN(S)

2. Grease inside of tin with white fat, then line the tin with greaseproof paper.

3. Grease the paper with white fat.

MAKING THE CAKE

4. Beat the butter and sugar until light, then stir in the ground almonds.

5. Lightly mix the eggs together. Then thoroughly beat in a small portion of egg at a time, until all egg is used. Carefully fold in the flour to form a batter.

6. Mix all fruit, rum, lemon zest and juice together. Then stir the mixed fruit into the batter until evenly dispersed.

7. Spread mixture into prepared tin(s).

8. Bake the cake in centre of oven (170°C/325°F or Gas Mark 3). (See baking and storage instructions on page 16).

CAKE COST SHEET

CAKE __Light Fruit__   NAME _____   BOOK _____   PAGE _____

DATE MADE _____   SIZE _____   SHAPE _____

A INGREDIENTS	Weight	Cost
Butter		
Caster Sugar		
Ground Almonds		
Fresh Egg		
Self Raising Flour		
Cherries (halved)		
Cherries (chopped)		
Currants		
Sultanas		
Mixed Peel		
Rum		
Lemon Zest & Juice		
	Subtotal **A** = £ _____	

C PRODUCTS	Used	Cost
Greaseproof Paper		
White Fat		
Waxed Paper		
	Subtotal **C** = £ _____	

D TIME TAKEN	Minutes
Weighing	
Preparing Tin	
Making The Cake	
Total	
Charge per minute	× p
Total	
LABOUR CHARGE	Subtotal **D** = £ _____

B HEAT
10% of ingredients' cost   Subtotal **B** = £ _____

Subtotals **A** + **B** + **C** + **D** =

TOTAL COST = £ _____

NOTE: Please refer to the information on pages 5–7 before attempting to complete this COST SHEET.
A 'MASTER' Cost Sheet can be found on page 114.

Ingredients

(USING APPROPRIATE SIZE TIN).

TIN SIZE	18cm (7in) SQUARE OR 20.5cm (8in) ROUND		20.5cm (8in) SQUARE OR 23cm (9in) ROUND		23cm (9in) SQUARE OR 25.5cm (10in) ROUND		25.5cm (10in) SQUARE OR 28cm (11in) ROUND		28cm (11in) SQUARE OR 30.5cm (12in) ROUND	
BUTTER	170g	6oz	225g	8oz	285g	10oz	340g	12oz	455g	16oz
CASTER SUGAR	170g	6oz	225g	8oz	285g	10oz	340g	12oz	455g	16oz
GROUND ALMONDS	45g	1½oz	60g	2oz	70g	2½oz	85g	3oz	115g	4oz
FRESH EGG	170g	6oz	225g	8oz	285g	10oz	340g	12oz	455g	16oz
SELF RAISING FLOUR	170g	6oz	225g	8oz	285g	10oz	340g	12oz	455g	16oz
CHERRIES (HALVED)	130g	4½oz	170g	6oz	215g	7½oz	255g	9oz	340g	12oz
CHERRIES (CHOPPED)	45g	1½oz	60g	2oz	75g	2½oz	85g	3oz	115g	4oz
CURRANTS	130g	4½oz	170g	6oz	215g	7½oz	255g	9oz	340g	12oz
SULTANAS	170g	6oz	225g	8oz	285g	10oz	340g	12oz	455g	16oz
MIXED PEEL	85g	3oz	115g	4oz	145g	5oz	170g	6oz	225g	8oz
RUM	22g	¾oz	30g	1oz	35g	1¼oz	45g	1½oz	60g	2oz
LEMON ZEST AND JUICE	¾ lemon		1 lemon		1¼ lemons		1½ lemons		2 lemons	

BAKING TIMES	2¼ hours	2½ hours	2¾ hours	3 hours	3¼ hours

Baking temperature 170°C/325°F or Gas Mark 3

FRUIT CAKE – BAKING INSTRUCTIONS

At the end of the recommended baking time, test the cake to ensure it is properly cooked by:
(a) bringing the cake forward from the oven;
(b) inserting a stainless steel skewer into the cake's centre;
(c) slowly raising skewer and, if clean, the cake is baked and should be removed from the oven; if mixture clings to the skewer, remove skewer and continue baking at the same temperature (test thereafter at ten minute intervals until the cake is baked).
After baking, leave cake in the tin until cool. Remove cake from tin and place on a wire tray. Leave until cold. See 'FRUIT CAKE – STORAGE' for further instructions.

NUMBER OF CAKE PORTIONS

To calculate size of fruit cake required, 8 portions are generally cut from 455g (16oz) of finished cake.

FRUIT CAKE – STORAGE

Wrap cake in waxed paper and store out of direct sunlight in a cool dry atmosphere which allows odourless air circulation.
If not stored correctly the cake could become mouldy because of:
(a) being wrapped whilst still warm;
(b) not using a good quality waxed paper to wrap the cake;
(c) being stored in the wrong temperature or in a variable temperature;
(d) the presence of moisture in the air;
(e) under-baking;
(f) too much soaking with alcohol after baking;
(g) leaving the cake too long before wrapping it in waxed paper.
DO NOT STORE cakes in sealed plastic containers, cling film or tin-foil.

To prevent cake cracking whilst being handled, wrap and then immediately place on a cake-board.

Almond Paste/Sugarpaste

MAKING ALMOND PASTE

CASTER SUGAR	170g	6oz
ICING SUGAR (SIEVED)	170g	6oz
GROUND ALMONDS	340g	12oz
GLUCOSE SYRUP	225g	8oz

MAKING SUGARPASTE

WATER	75g	2½oz
POWDERED GELATINE	15g	½oz
GLUCOSE SYRUP	75g	2½oz
GLYCERINE	75g	2½oz
ICING SUGAR (SIEVED)	710g	1lb 9oz

MAKING SUGARPASTE
STEPS 1–4

TIME

STARTED   _____

FINISHED   _____

TIME TAKEN   _____

MAKING ALMOND PASTE
STEPS 1–2

TIME

STARTED   _____

FINISHED   _____

TIME TAKEN   _____

1. Mix all dry ingredients together. Warm and pour in the glucose.

1. Pour the water into a non-stick saucepan. Sprinkle the gelatine on the water.

2. Mix together to form a pliable paste. Store in sealed container until required. Note: The consistency of the paste can be altered by adjusting the quantity of glucose.

2. Dissolve the gelatine by heating gently. Stir in the glucose and glycerine, then remove from heat.

WORK NOTES

3. Pour solution into a mixing bowl, then slowly add and mix in the icing sugar.

4. Continue mixing until a pliable paste is formed. Store in a polythene bag until required. This paste is ideal for covering cakes.

ALMOND PASTE COST SHEET

DATE MADE _____

A INGREDIENTS	Weight	Cost
Caster Sugar	_____	_____
Icing Sugar (sieved)	_____	_____
Ground Almonds	_____	_____
Glucose Syrup	_____	_____
	_____	_____
	_____	_____
	_____	_____
	Subtotal A = £ _____

B TIME TAKEN	Minutes
Making	_____
	_____
Total	_____
Charge per Minute	× p
Total	_____
LABOUR CHARGE	Subtotal B = £ _____

Subtotals **A** + **B** = **TOTAL COST** = £ _____
TOTAL WEIGHT _____

SUGAR PASTE COST SHEET

DATE MADE _____

A INGREDIENTS	Weight	Cost
Water	_____	_____
Powdered Gelatine	_____	_____
Glucose Syrup	_____	_____
Icing Sugar (sieved)	_____	_____
	_____	_____
	_____	_____
	_____	_____
	Subtotal A = £ _____

B TIME TAKEN	Minutes
Making	_____
	_____
Total	_____
Charge per Minute	× p
Total	_____
LABOUR CHARGE	Subtotal B = £ _____

Subtotals **A** + **B** = **TOTAL COST** = £ _____
TOTAL WEIGHT (approx) _____

NOTE: Please refer to the information on pages 5–8 before attempting to complete this COST SHEET. A 'MASTER' Cost Sheet can be found on page 114.

Buttercream/Royal Icing

MAKING BUTTERCREAM

BUTTER	285g	10oz
ICING SUGAR (SIEVED)	570g	1lb 4oz
WARM WATER	60g	2oz

Note: When making buttercream all the ingredients should be 18°C/65°F.

1. Beat the butter until light.

2. Gradually add the icing sugar (beating well after each addition). Then thoroughly beat in the water. Store in a refrigerator until required.

MAKING ROYAL ICING

PURE ALBUMEN POWDER	22g	¾oz
WATER	145g	5oz
ICING SUGAR (SIEVED)	740g	1lb 10oz

1. Briskly stir the albumen powder into the water. Leave to dissolve for 1 hour. (Stir occasionally during this time.)

2. Strain the solution into a machine bowl through muslin or a fine sieve.

3. Stir in a third of the icing sugar and beat for 2 minutes.

MAKING BUTTERCREAM
STEPS 1–2

TIME

STARTED   _____

FINISHED   _____

TIME TAKEN   _____

MAKING ROYAL ICING
STEPS 1–4

TIME

STARTED   _____

FINISHED   _____

TIME TAKEN   _____

(Do not include solution standing time)

WORK NOTES

4. Carefully mix in remaining icing sugar and then beat until a light, firm consistency is formed. Store in sealed container until required.

GLYCERINE
TABLE FOR USE

FOR SOFT-CUTTING ROYAL ICING ADD THE FOLLOWING AMOUNTS OF GLYCERINE TO EACH

455g (16oz)
OF READY-MADE ROYAL ICING:-

1 TEASPOON
FOR BOTTOM TIER OF A THREE TIER CAKE.

2 TEASPOONS
FOR MIDDLE TIER OF A THREE TIER CAKE, OR THE BOTTOM TIER OF A TWO TIER CAKE.

3 TEASPOONS
FOR TOP TIER OR SINGLE TIER CAKE.

GLYCERINE MUST NOT BE ADDED TO ROYAL ICING WHICH IS BEING USED FOR RUNOUTS, FIGURE PIPING OR FINE LINE WORK.

BUTTERCREAM COST SHEET

DATE MADE _____

A INGREDIENTS	Weight	Cost
Butter		
Icing Sugar (sieved)		
Warm water		
	Subtotal **A** = £ _____

B TIME TAKEN	Minutes
Making	
Total	_____
Charge per Minute	× p
Total	_____
LABOUR CHARGE	Subtotal **B** = £ _____

Subtotals **A** + **B** = **TOTAL COST** = £ _____

TOTAL WEIGHT _____

ROYAL ICING COST SHEET

DATE MADE _____

A INGREDIENTS	Weight	Cost
Pure Albumen Powder		
Water		
Icing Sugar (sieved)		
	Subtotal **A** = £ _____

B TIME TAKEN	Minutes
Making	
Total	_____
Charge per Minute	× p
Total	_____
LABOUR CHARGE	Subtotal **B** = £ _____

Subtotals **A** + **B** = **TOTAL COST** = £ _____

TOTAL WEIGHT (approx) _____

NOTE: Please refer to the information on pages 5–8 before attempting to complete this COST SHEET. A 'MASTER' Cost Sheet can be found on page 114.

Making Flower Paste

WORK NOTES

MAKING FLOWER PASTE
STEPS 1–6

TIME

STARTED   ———

FINISHED   ———

TIME TAKEN   ———

FLOWER PASTE IS A FIRM, SWEET PASTE WHICH IS GENERALLY USED FOR MODELLING HAND-MADE CAKE ARTISTRY FLOWERS.

2. Sieve the dry ingredients into a mixing bowl. Sieve three times.

CORNFLOUR	60g	2oz
ICING SUGAR (SIEVED)	400g	14oz
GUM TRAGACANTH	22g	¾oz
GLUCOSE SYRUP	22g	¾oz
COLD WATER	60g	2oz
WHITE FAT	22g	¾oz

3. Pour in remaining ingredients.

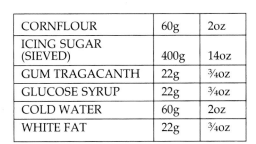

MAKING FLOWER PASTE
1. Weigh all the dry ingredients carefully on to greaseproof paper.

4. Thoroughly mix the ingredients (using a machine on 'slow' or by hand with a wooden spoon).

WORK NOTES

5. The paste is properly mixed when 'clear' and does not stick to the side of the bowl.

6. Mould the paste into a ball and place in a polythene bag. Leave to mature for at least 24 hours.

FLOWER PASTE ROSE

FLOWER PASTE COST SHEET		
DATE MADE		
A INGREDIENTS	Weight	Cost
Cornflour		
Icing Sugar (sieved)		
Gum Tragacanth		
Glucose Syrup		
Water		
White Fat		
	Subtotal **A** = £	
B TIME TAKEN	Minutes	
Making		
Total		
Charge per Minute	× p	
Total		
LABOUR CHARGE	Subtotal **B** = £	
Subtotals **A** + **B** = **TOTAL COST** = £		
TOTAL WEIGHT		

NOTE: Please refer to the information on pages 5–8 before attempting to complete this COST SHEET
A 'MASTER' Cost Sheet can be found on page 115.

FILLING AND COATING A GENOESE SPONGE CAKE WITH BUTTERCREAM

FLAVOURING
BUTTERCREAM
STEP 1

TIME

STARTED   _____

FINISHED   _____

TIME TAKEN   _____

FILLING AND FIRST
COATING
STEPS 2–5

TIME

STARTED   _____

FINISHED   _____

TIME TAKEN   _____

FLAVOURING BUTTERCREAM
1. Beat chosen flavour and colour into buttercream.

EXAMPLE 'A'

BUTTERCREAM	455g	16oz
MELTED CHOCOLATE	115g	4oz

EXAMPLE 'B'

BUTTERCREAM	455g	16oz
ORANGE/LEMON JUICE (TO TASTE)		
ORANGE/LEMON (FOOD COLOURING)		

3. Place one layer of sponge on a cake-card and then coat top with buttercream.

4. Place remaining layer on top. Coat top with buttercream.

FILLING AND FIRST COATING
2. Remove crusts from the sponge top, bottom and side. Slice the sponge in half.

5. Spread buttercream around sponge side and then neaten the top edge with a palette knife. Leave in a refrigerator for 1 hour.

WORK NOTES

SECOND COATING
STEPS 6–7

TIME

STARTED _____

FINISHED _____

TIME TAKEN _____

SECOND COATING
6. Coat sponge with a second layer of buttercream.

7. Neaten edge, as shown, to complete the coating. Decorate as required.

COATED CAKE COST SHEET

DATE _____ NAME _____ BOOK _____
PAGE _____ SIZE _____ SHAPE _____
CAKE __Genoese__ COVERING _____ COATING __Buttercream__

A PRODUCTS	Used	Cost
Genoese Sponge	___	___
Cake-Card	___	___
Buttercream	___	___
Flavour	___	___
Colour	___	___
___	___	___
___	___	___
___	___	___
___	___	___
___	___	___
___	___	___
	Subtotal **A** = £ ___	

B TIME TAKEN	Minutes
Flavour Buttercream	___
Fill & 1st Coat	___
2nd Coat	___
___	___
___	___
___	___
___	___
___	___
Total	___
Charge per minute × p	
Total	___
LABOUR CHARGE Subtotal **B** = £ ___	

Subtotals **A** + **B** = **TOTAL COST** = £ ___

NOTE: Please refer to the information on pages 5–9 before attempting to complete this COST SHEET.
A 'MASTER' Cost Sheet can be found on page 116.

COVERING A LIGHT FRUIT CAKE WITH ALMOND PASTE AND SUGARPASTE

COVERING CAKE WITH ALMOND PASTE

1. Place cake on a cake board. Fill in any surface imperfections with almond paste. Brush cake-top and side with boiling apricot purée.

4. Cut surplus almond paste from cake base, then smooth top and side with a cake smoother. Leave to dry for 24 hours.

2. Roll out almond paste and lay over the cake.

COVERING CAKE WITH SUGARPASTE

5. Colour and flavour sugarpaste. Brush entire surface of almond paste with cooled boiled water or liqueur of choice.

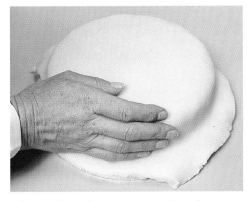

3. Press almond paste against the cake-top and side, using palm of hand.

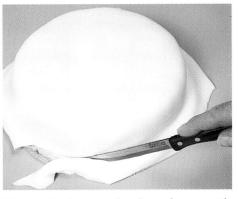

6. Immediately cover the almond paste with a thin layer of the sugarpaste. Trim surplus from cake base.

WORK NOTES

7. Smooth the sugarpaste with a cake smoother, whilst using a cake scraper at the back to support the cake.

8. Leave to dry for 24 hours. Decorate as required.

COATED CAKE COST SHEET

DATE _____ NAME _____ BOOK _____

PAGE _____ SIZE _____ SHAPE _____

CAKE __Light Fruit__ COVERING __Almond Paste__ COATING __Sugarpaste__

A PRODUCTS	Used	Cost	B TIME TAKEN	Minutes
Fruit Cake	____	____	Covering with A.P.	____
Cake-Board	____	____	Covering with S.P.	____
Almond Paste	____	____		
Apricot Purée	____	____		
Sugarpaste	____	____		
Colour	____	____		
____	____	____		
____	____	____		
____	____	____	Total	____
____	____	____	Charge per minute	× p
____	____	____	Total	____
____	____	____	LABOUR CHARGE Subtotal **B** = £ ____	
____	____	____	Subtotals **A** + **B** = **TOTAL COST** = £ ____	
	Subtotal **A** = £ ____			

NOTE: Please refer to the information on pages 5–8 before attempting to complete this COST SHEET.
A 'MASTER' Cost Sheet can be found on page 116.

COVERING A LIGHT FRUIT CAKE WITH ALMOND PASTE AND COATING WITH ROYAL ICING

COVERING WITH
ALMOND PASTE
STEPS 1–3

TIME

STARTED   _____

FINISHED   _____

TIME TAKEN   _____

FIRST COATING – TOP
STEP 4

TIME

STARTED   _____

FINISHED   _____

TIME TAKEN   _____

FIRST COATING – SIDES
STEP 5

TIME

STARTED   _____

FINISHED   _____

TIME TAKEN   _____

SECOND COATING – TOP
AND SIDES
STEP 6

TIME

STARTED   _____

FINISHED   _____

TIME TAKEN   _____

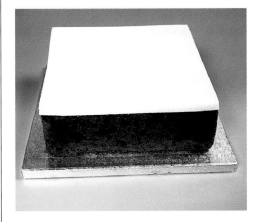

COVERING CAKE WITH ALMOND PASTE

1. Invert a matured fruit cake on to a cake board. Brush boiling apricot purée on cake-top and cover with almond paste.

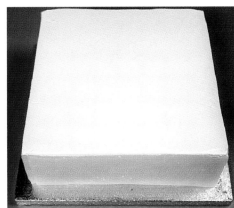

FIRST COATING – TOP

4. Coat the cake-top with royal icing – using the glycerine table on page 20. Leave to dry for 12 hours.

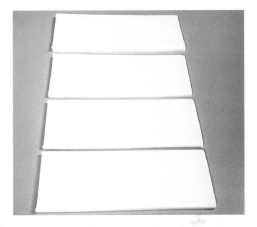

2. Roll out and cut four strips of almond paste for cake sides.

FIRST COATING – SIDES

5. Coat the cake sides with royal icing. Leave to dry for 12 hours.

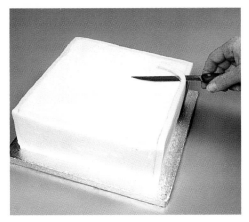

3. Fix a strip to each side, using boiling apricot purée. Trim off surplus from the cake edges. Leave to dry for 24 hours.

SECOND COATING – TOP AND SIDES

6. Coat the cake-top and sides with royal icing. Leave to dry for 12 hours.

Light Fruit Cake with Almond Paste and Coating with Royal Icing

WORK NOTES

THIRD COATING – TOP
AND SIDES
STEP 7

TIME

STARTED   _____

FINISHED   _____

TIME TAKEN   _____

COATING BOARD
STEP 8

TIME

STARTED   _____

FINISHED   _____

TIME TAKEN   _____

THIRD COATING – TOP AND SIDES

7. Coat the cake-top and sides with royal icing. Leave to dry for 12 hours.

COATING BOARD

8. If required, coat top of cake-board to complete the coating. Leave to dry 12 hours.

COATED CAKE COST SHEET

DATE _____   NAME _____   BOOK _____

PAGE _____   SIZE _____   SHAPE _____

CAKE __**Light Fruit**__   COVERING __**Almond Paste**__   COATING __**Royal Icing**__

A PRODUCTS	Used	Cost	B TIME TAKEN	Minutes
Light Fruit Cake			**Covering with A.P.**	
Cake-Board			**1st Coat Top**	
Almond Paste			**1st Coat Sides**	
Apricot Purée			**2nd Coat Top & Sides**	
Royal Icing			**3rd Coat Top & Sides**	
Glycerine			**Coating Board**	
			Total	_____
			Charge per minute × p	
			Total	_____
			LABOUR CHARGE Subtotal **B** = £ _____	
		Subtotals **A** + **B** =	**TOTAL COST** = £ _____	
	Subtotal **A** = £ _____			

NOTE: Please refer to the information on pages 5–10 before attempting to complete this COST SHEET.
A 'MASTER' Cost Sheet can be found on page 116.

CHERRY'S CAKE PROFILE
OCCASION – CELEBRATION

CAKE	–	GENOESE SPONGE			PAGE 13
SHAPE	–	ROUND	20.5cm	8in	
BOARD	–	ROUND	20.5cm	8in	
FILLING	–	BUTTERCREAM	115g	4oz	PAGE 19
COATING	–	BUTTERCREAM	455g	16oz	PAGE 19
PIPING	–	BUTTERCREAM	60g	2oz	PAGE 19

WORK NOTES

DECORATING THE CAKE
STEPS 1–8

TIME

STARTED   ———

FINISHED   ———

TIME TAKEN   ———

DECORATING THE CAKE

1. A sponge cake coated with chocolate-flavoured buttercream, is required. Cover side with roasted chopped nuts.

4. Pipe melted chocolate around the cake-top, as shown.

2. Carefully place a pastry cutter on the cake-top centre.

5. Pipe rosettes around edge of nuts on the cake-top centre (No. 7).

3. Sprinkle chopped nuts evenly inside the cutter, then carefully remove the cutter.

6. Pipe rosettes around cake-top edge, as shown (No. 7).

7. Fix a jelly diamond to each rosette on the cake-top centre.

8. Cut and fix half a cherry to each outer edge rosette.

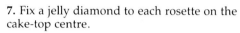

COST SUMMARY

DATE _____ NAME _____ BOOK _____
PAGE _____ SIZE _____ SHAPE _____
CAKE _____ COVERING _____ COATING _____

A PRODUCTS	Used	Cost
_____	_____	_____
_____	_____	_____
_____	_____	_____
_____	_____	_____
_____	_____	_____
_____	_____	_____
_____	_____	_____
_____	_____	_____
_____	_____	_____
_____	_____	_____
_____	_____	_____
_____	_____	_____
_____	_____	_____
_____	_____	_____
_____	_____	_____
_____	_____	_____
	Subtotal: **A** = £ _____	

B TIME TAKEN	Minutes
_____	_____
_____	_____
_____	_____
_____	_____
_____	_____
_____	_____
_____	_____
_____	_____
_____	_____
Total	_____
Charge per minute	× p
Total	_____
LABOUR CHARGE Subtotal **B** =	£ _____

Subtotals **A** + **B** = TOTAL COST = £ _____
OVERHEAD COSTS = £ _____
PROFIT COSTS = £ _____
GRAND TOTAL = £ _____

NOTE: Please refer to the information on pages 5–10 before attempting to complete this COST SHEET.
A 'MASTER' Cost Sheet can be found on page 116.

$Adam$

ADAM'S CAKE PROFILE
OCCASION – BIRTHDAY

CAKE	–	GENOESE SPONGE			PAGE 13
SHAPE	–	ROUND	20.5cm	8in	
BOARD	–	ROUND	20.5cm	8in	
FILLING	–	BUTTERCREAM	115g	4oz	PAGE 19
COVERING	–	BUTTERCREAM	115g	4oz	PAGE 19
COATING	–	SUGARPASTE	115g	4oz	PAGE 17
PIPING	–	ROYAL ICING	115g	4oz	PAGE 19

1. Picture showing sponge cake, covered in buttercream, on its cake-card.

DECORATING THE CAKE
2. Roll out, cut and fix a sugarpaste disc to the cake-top.

3. Cover the side with roasted flaked almonds.

4. Pipe inscription of choice on cake-top (No. 1).

5. Decorate inscription with piped lines and dots, as shown (No. 1).

6. Pipe shells around the cake-top edge (No. 44).

DECORATING THE CAKE
STEPS 2–8

TIME

STARTED   _____

FINISHED   _____

TIME TAKEN   _____

WORK NOTES

7. Pipe a dot between each shell (No. 1).

8. Fix artificial decorations to the cake-top, as required.

COST SUMMARY

DATE _____ NAME _____ BOOK _____

PAGE _____ SIZE _____ SHAPE _____

CAKE _____ COVERING _____ COATING _____

A PRODUCTS	Used	Cost
_____	_____	_____
_____	_____	_____
_____	_____	_____
_____	_____	_____
_____	_____	_____
_____	_____	_____
_____	_____	_____
_____	_____	_____
_____	_____	_____
_____	_____	_____
_____	_____	_____
_____	_____	_____
_____	_____	_____
_____	_____	_____
_____	_____	_____
_____	_____	_____
_____	_____	_____
_____	_____	_____
		Subtotal: **A** = £ _____

B TIME TAKEN   Minutes

_____

_____

_____

_____

_____

_____

_____

_____

_____

Total _____

Charge per minute   ×   p

Total _____

LABOUR CHARGE   Subtotal **B** = £ _____

Subtotals **A** + **B** = TOTAL COST = £ _____

OVERHEAD COSTS = £ _____

PROFIT COSTS = £ _____

GRAND TOTAL = £ _____

NOTE: Please refer to the information on pages 5–10 before attempting to complete this COST SHEET.
A 'MASTER' Cost Sheet can be found on page 116.

Jumbo

JUMBO'S CAKE PROFILE
OCCASION – BIRTHDAY

CAKE	– GENOESE SPONGE			PAGE 13
SHAPE	– ROUND	20.5cm	8in	
BOARD	– ROUND	30.5cm	12in	
FILLING	– JAM	60g	2oz	
COVERING	– BUTTERCREAM	115g	4oz	PAGE 19
COATING	– SUGARPASTE	455g	16oz	PAGE 17
PIPING	– ROYAL ICING	60g	2oz	PAGE 19

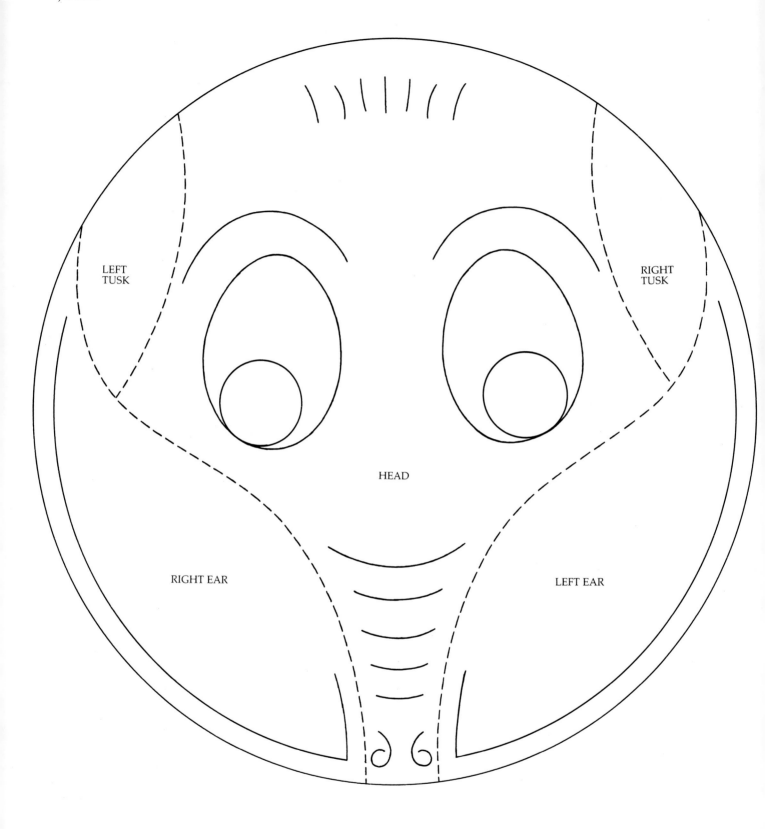

LEFT
TUSK

RIGHT
TUSK

HEAD

RIGHT EAR

LEFT EAR

JUMBO'S TEMPLATE
FOR 20.5cm (8in) ROUND CAKE

WORK NOTES

MAKING THE TEMPLATE
STEP 1

TIME

STARTED   _____

FINISHED   _____

TIME TAKEN   _____

DECORATING THE CAKE
STEPS 2–7

TIME

STARTED   _____

FINISHED   _____

TIME TAKEN   _____

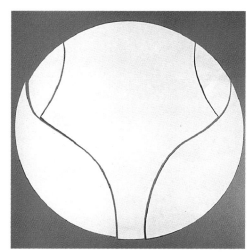

MAKING THE TEMPLATE

1. Trace Jumbo's template on to plain card. Cut along the dotted lines to form the various shapes shown.

4. Coat the top and sides of each piece with a thin layer of buttercream.

DECORATING THE CAKE

2. Slice a sponge in half, fill with jam of choice and sandwich together.

5. Cover each piece with sugarpaste, then arrange on the doyley and board, to form 'Jumbo'.

3. Using each template as a guide, cut the sponge into the pieces shown.

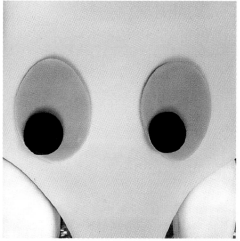

6. Roll out, cut and fix sugarpaste eyes.

Jumbo

WORK NOTES

MAKING THE PENNANT
STEP 8

TIME

STARTED _____

FINISHED _____

TIME TAKEN _____

7. Pipe the feature lines shown (No. 2).

MAKING THE PENNANT
8. Make the pennant from a drinking straw and paper. Pipe inscription of choice (No. 1) on pennant and then fix to cake-board in a sugarpaste base.

COST SUMMARY

DATE _____ NAME _____ BOOK _____

PAGE _____ SIZE _____ SHAPE _____

CAKE _____ COVERING _____ COATING _____

A PRODUCTS	Used	Cost
_____	_____	_____
_____	_____	_____
_____	_____	_____
_____	_____	_____
_____	_____	_____
_____	_____	_____
_____	_____	_____
_____	_____	_____
_____	_____	_____
_____	_____	_____
_____	_____	_____
_____	_____	_____
_____	_____	_____
_____	_____	_____
_____	_____	_____
_____	_____	_____
_____	_____	_____
_____	_____	_____
_____	_____	_____
	Subtotal: **A** = £ _____	

B TIME TAKEN	Minutes
_____	_____
_____	_____
_____	_____
_____	_____
_____	_____
_____	_____
_____	_____
_____	_____
_____	_____
_____	_____
_____	_____
Total	_____
Charge per minute	× p
Total	_____
LABOUR CHARGE Subtotal **B** =	£ _____

Subtotals **A** + **B** = TOTAL COST = £ _____

OVERHEAD COSTS = £ _____

PROFIT COSTS = £ _____

GRAND TOTAL = £ _____

NOTE: Please refer to the information on pages 5–10 before attempting to complete this COST SHEET. A 'MASTER' Cost Sheet can be found on page 116.

Sophia

SOPHIA'S CAKE PROFILE
OCCASION – CELEBRATION

CAKE	–	GENOESE SPONGE			PAGE 13
SHAPE	–	ROUND	20.5cm	8in	
BOARD	–	ROUND	25.5cm	10in	
FILLING	–	BUTTERCREAM	60g	2oz	PAGE 19
COVERING	–	BUTTERCREAM	115g	4oz	PAGE 19
COATING	–	SUGARPASTE	455g	16oz	PAGE 17
PIPING	–	ROYAL ICING	115g	4oz	PAGE 19

Sophia

DECORATING THE CAKE
STEPS 2–8

TIME

STARTED   _____

FINISHED   _____

TIME TAKEN   _____

1. Picture showing sponge cake, covered in buttercream, on its board.

4. Roll out, cut and fix a sugarpaste ribbon over the cake.

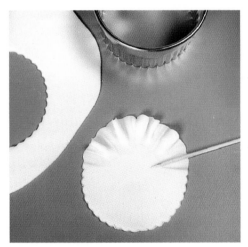

DECORATING THE CAKE

2. Roll out and cut a fluted disc of sugarpaste. Frill the edge by rolling a cocktail stick backwards and forwards a little at a time. 5 different sized discs required.

5. Pipe a line to form flower stem (No. 3). Roll out, cut and fix sugarpaste leaves to the stem.

3. Fix each disc together on cake-top to form the flower head. Decorate centre of flower, as shown.

6. Pipe bulbs around the cake base (No. 3).

7. Overpipe each bulb with a piped line (No. 2). Then overpipe each line (No. 1).

8. Pipe inscription of choice on the ribbon (No. 1). Fix artificial decorations of choice to the cake-top.

COST SUMMARY

DATE _____   NAME _____   BOOK _____
PAGE _____   SIZE _____   SHAPE _____
CAKE _____   COVERING _____   COATING _____

A PRODUCTS	Used	Cost
_____	_____	_____
_____	_____	_____
_____	_____	_____
_____	_____	_____
_____	_____	_____
_____	_____	_____
_____	_____	_____
_____	_____	_____
_____	_____	_____
_____	_____	_____
_____	_____	_____
_____	_____	_____
_____	_____	_____
_____	_____	_____
_____	_____	_____

Subtotal: **A** = £ _____

B TIME TAKEN	Minutes
_____	_____
_____	_____
_____	_____
_____	_____
_____	_____
_____	_____
_____	_____
_____	_____
_____	_____
_____	_____

Total _____
Charge per minute   × p
Total _____
LABOUR CHARGE   Subtotal **B** = £ _____

Subtotals **A** + **B** = TOTAL COST =   £ _____
OVERHEAD COSTS =   £ _____
PROFIT COSTS =   £ _____
GRAND TOTAL =   £ _____

NOTE: Please refer to the information on pages 5–10 before attempting to complete this COST SHEET.
A 'MASTER' Cost Sheet can be found on page 116.

GLEN'S CAKE PROFILE
OCCASION – BIRTHDAY

CAKE	–	GENOESE SPONGE			PAGE 13
SHAPE	–	SQUARE	20.5cm	8in	
BOARD	–	SQUARE	30.5cm	12in	
FILLING	–	BUTTERCREAM	85g	3oz	PAGE 19
COVERING	–	BUTTERCREAM	115g	4oz	PAGE 19
COATING	–	SUGARPASTE	680g	1lb 8oz	PAGE 17
PIPING	–	ROYAL ICING	225g	8oz	PAGE 19

WORK NOTES

DECORATING THE CAKE
STEPS 2–8

TIME

STARTED   ————

FINISHED   ————

TIME TAKEN   ————

1. Picture showing sponge cake, covered in buttercream on its board.

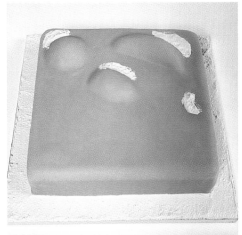

4. Stipple cake-board and the parts of the cake-top shown with royal icing.

DECORATING THE CAKE
2. Shape and fix sugarpaste pieces to the cake-top to form mounds.

5. Stipple the further parts of the cake-top shown. Pipe shells around the cake-base (No. 43).

3. Cover cake-top and sides with one sheet of sugarpaste.

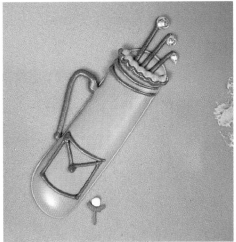

6. Outline and flood-in a bag of golf-clubs on the cake-top, using the picture as a guide.

WORK NOTES

7. Fix artificial flags and figures of golfers to the cake-top.

8. Press sugarpaste through a wire sieve, to form bushes. Fix bushes on the cake-top and board. Make and fix a sugarpaste plaque.

COST SUMMARY

DATE _____ NAME _____ BOOK _____

PAGE _____ SIZE _____ SHAPE _____

CAKE _____ COVERING _____ COATING _____

A PRODUCTS	Used	Cost

Subtotal: **A** = £ _____

B TIME TAKEN	Minutes

Total _____

Charge per minute × p

Total _____

LABOUR CHARGE   Subtotal **B** = £ _____

Subtotals **A** + **B** = TOTAL COST = £ _____

OVERHEAD COSTS = £ _____

PROFIT COSTS = £ _____

GRAND TOTAL = £ _____

NOTE: Please refer to the information on pages 5–10 before attempting to complete this COST SHEET. A 'MASTER' Cost Sheet can be found on page 116.

Vivienne

VIVIENNE'S CAKE PROFILE
OCCASION – ANNIVERSARY

CAKE	–	FRUIT CAKE			PAGE 16
SHAPE	–	ROUND	20.5cm	8in	
BOARD	–	ROUND	28cm	11in	
COVERING	–	ALMOND PASTE	455g	16oz	PAGE 17
COATING	–	SUGARPASTE	680g	1lb 8oz	PAGE 17
PIPING	–	ROYAL ICING	60g	2oz	PAGE 19
ROSES	–	SUGARPASTE	225g	8oz	PAGE 17

WORK NOTES

MAKING ROSES AND
LEAVES
STEPS 1–6

TIME

STARTED   _____

FINISHED   _____

TIME TAKEN   _____

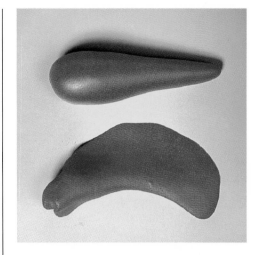

MAKING ROSES AND LEAVES

1. (a) Roll out sugarpaste to form a carrot shape. (b) Flatten one side as shown.

4. Make and fix further petals as required to form full blooms. Leave to dry for 12 hours, then remove surplus sugarpaste.

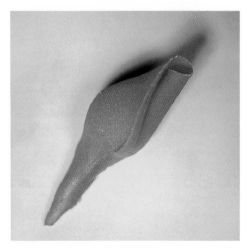

2. Immediately roll the sugarpaste from right to left to form a rosebud. Remove any surplus sugarpaste.

5. Roll out, cut and vein sugarpaste leaves.

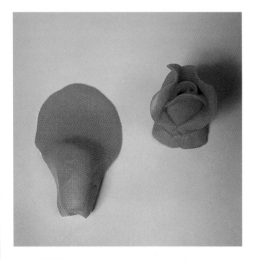

3. (a) Roll out sugarpaste, then flatten one end to make a petal. Fix and fold petal around the rose bud. (b) Repeat '(a)' twice more.

6. Three roses, four rosebuds and seven leaves are required. Leave to dry for 24 hours.

WORK NOTES

MAKING A CARD
STEP 7

TIME

STARTED   ———

FINISHED   ———

TIME TAKEN   ———

DECORATING THE CAKE
STEPS 9–14

TIME

STARTED   ———

FINISHED   ———

TIME TAKEN   ———

MAKING A CARD
7. Roll out and cut a sugarpaste card. Decorate with royal icing as shown (No. 1). Leave to dry for 24 hours.

10. Join each heart with piped lines and dots (No. 1).

8. Picture showing coated cake and coated board (the latter with a crimped edge).

11. Fix roses to cake-top, as shown.

DECORATING THE CAKE
9. Pipe heart motifs around cake-top edge (No. 1).

12. Fix rosebuds and leaves to form a spray.

WORK NOTES

13. Fix rosebuds and leaves on cake-base, then ribbon to cake-board edge.

14. Fix the sugarpaste card to the cake-top.

COST SUMMARY

DATE _____ NAME _____ BOOK _____
PAGE _____ SIZE _____ SHAPE _____
CAKE _____ COVERING _____ COATING _____

A PRODUCTS	Used	Cost
	Subtotal: **A** = £ _____	

B TIME TAKEN	Minutes
	Total _____

Charge per minute   ×   p

Total _____

LABOUR CHARGE   Subtotal **B** = £ _____

Subtotals **A** + **B** = TOTAL COST =   £ _____
OVERHEAD COSTS =   £ _____
PROFIT COSTS =   £ _____
GRAND TOTAL =   £ _____

NOTE: Please refer to the information on pages 5–10 before attempting to complete this COST SHEET.
A 'MASTER' Cost Sheet can be found on page 116.

<table>
<tr><td colspan="2" align="center">Spring</td></tr>
</table>

SPRING'S CAKE PROFILE
OCCASION – EASTER

CAKE	–	FRUIT CAKE			PAGE 16
SHAPE	–	PETAL	20.5cm	8in	
BOARD	–	ROUND	30.5cm	12in	
COVERING	–	ALMOND PASTE	455g	16oz	PAGE 17
COATING	–	SUGARPASTE	680g	1lb 8oz	PAGE 17
PIPING	–	ROYAL ICING	115g	4oz	PAGE 19
DAFFODILS	–	FLOWER PASTE	115g	4oz	PAGE 21

49

WORK NOTES

MAKING FLOWER HEADS
STEPS 2–5

TIME

STARTED   _____

FINISHED   _____

TIME TAKEN   _____

MAKING THE STEMS
STEPS 6–10

TIME

STARTED   _____

FINISHED   _____

TIME TAKEN   _____

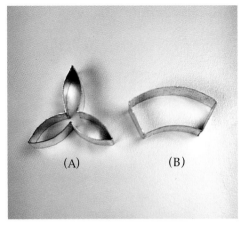

1. Daffodil petal cutter (A) and trumpet cutter (B) required.

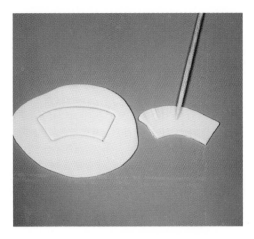

4. Roll out and cut the shape shown from sugarpaste, using cutter (B). Frill the longer (outer) edge by rolling a cocktail stick backwards and forwards a little at a time.

MAKING FLOWER HEADS
2. Roll out and cut two flower paste petal shapes – using cutter (A). Place on a dry household sponge and thin the edges. Mark each petal with a cocktail stick, as shown.

5. Moisten one end of the shape with egg white. Join end to end to form a trumpet. Moisten base of trumpet and fix to the petals. Leave to dry for 24 hours. 2 flowers are required.

3. Moisten the centre of one of the petal shapes with egg white. Immediately join the shapes together to form a flower. Pierce the flower centre with a cocktail stick.

MAKING THE STEMS
6. (a) Cut and bend a length of lime green 24 gauge wire, as shown. (b) Loop and twist wire over six stamen heads. (c) Fix together in upright position using floral tape.

WORK NOTES

MAKING THE LEAVES
STEP 11

TIME

STARTED   ————

FINISHED   ————

TIME TAKEN   ————

COMPLETING THE SPRAY
STEP 12

TIME

STARTED   ————

FINISHED   ————

TIME TAKEN   ————

7. Mould a ball of flower paste and insert stem through it. Moisten the inside centre of the flower and insert the stem through the existing hole.

10. Wind white floral tape around the stem, as shown, then coat the tape with edible confectioners' dusting powder.

8. Pull the stem through the flower until the flower paste ball and stamen heads are in the position shown. Then use a cocktail stick to flatten the flower paste ball.

MAKING THE LEAVES
11. Cut out and mark two flower paste leaves. Insert a length of 26 gauge wire into the base of each leaf and then leave to dry, in the shape shown for 24 hours.

9. Mould a cone of flower paste and insert the stem through its centre. Moisten the flower base with egg white and fix cone as shown. Leave to dry for 24 hours.

COMPLETING THE SPRAY
12. To form the spray, place the wired leaves against the flower stems and wrap together with floral tape.

13. Picture showing coated cake on its board.

DECORATING THE CAKE
14. Stipple the board-top with royal icing.

DECORATING THE CAKE
STEPS 14–20

TIME

STARTED   ————

FINISHED   ————

TIME TAKEN   ————

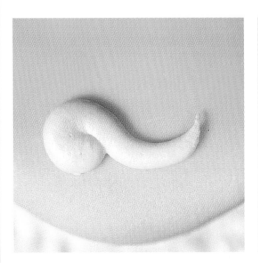

15. Pipe the shape shown on each petal section, to form rabbit bodies (No. 4).

16. Pipe heads and ears (No. 4), then pipe eyes and tails (No. 1), as shown.

17. Pipe grass (No. 1) beside each rabbit.

18. Pipe grass and rabbits (No. 2) around the cake base.

19. Fix the daffodil spray on to the cake-top. Then make and fix a ribbon bow, as shown.

20. Pipe and then decorate inscription of choice on cake-top (No. 1). Fix ribbon around cake-board edge.

COST SUMMARY

DATE _____ NAME _____ BOOK _____
PAGE _____ SIZE _____ SHAPE _____
CAKE _____ COVERING _____ COATING _____

A PRODUCTS	Used	Cost
	Subtotal: **A** = £ _____

B TIME TAKEN	Minutes
Total	_____
Charge per minute	× p
Total	_____
LABOUR CHARGE	Subtotal **B** = £ _____

Subtotals **A** + **B** = TOTAL COST = £ _____
OVERHEAD COSTS = £ _____
PROFIT COSTS = £ _____
GRAND TOTAL = £ _____

NOTE: Please refer to the information on pages 5–10 before attempting to complete this COST SHEET.
A 'MASTER' Cost Sheet can be found on page 116.

Joanna

JOANNA'S CAKE PROFILE
OCCASION – BIRTHDAY

CAKE	– GENOESE SPONGE			PAGE 13
SHAPE	– ROUND	20.5cm	8in	
BOARD	– ROUND	28cm	11in	
FILLING	– BUTTERCREAM	60g	2oz	PAGE 19
COVERING	– BUTTERCREAM	115g	4oz	PAGE 19
COATING	– SUGARPASTE	170g	6oz	PAGE 17
PIPING	– ROYAL ICING	115g	4oz	PAGE 19
DECORATION	– SUGARPASTE	115g	4oz	PAGE 17

MAKING THE TEDDY BEAR
1. Mould and fix sugarpaste body and head together, as shown.

MAKING THE FLOWERS
4. Roll out, cut and press fluted discs of sugarpaste on to a dry household sponge, to form flowers. Place each flower on waxed paper. Leave to dry for 2 hours.

WORK NOTES

MAKING THE TEDDY BEAR
STEPS 1–3

TIME

STARTED ＿＿＿＿＿

FINISHED ＿＿＿＿＿

TIME TAKEN ＿＿＿＿＿

MAKING THE FLOWERS
STEPS 4–5

TIME

STARTED ＿＿＿＿＿

FINISHED ＿＿＿＿＿

TIME TAKEN ＿＿＿＿＿

2. Mould and fix legs, arms and ears to body and head, to form a teddy bear.

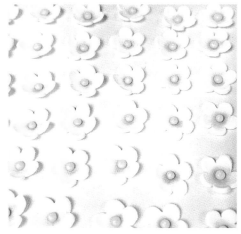

5. Brush the centre of each flower with confectioners' dusting powder. Then pipe a dot (No. 1) at each centre, as shown.

3. Mould and fix the nose. Decorate Teddy with piped royal icing (No. 1), then tie a ribbon and bow around neck. Leave to dry for 2 hours.

6. Picture showing the coated cake (with combed side) on its doyley and board.

55

WORK NOTES

DECORATING THE CAKE
STEPS 7–14

TIME

STARTED _____

FINISHED _____

TIME TAKEN _____

DECORATING THE CAKE
7. Pipe shells around cake base (No. 2) and then 'C' scrolls around the cake-top edge (No. 7).

10. Pipe graduated dots beside each scroll, as shown (No. 1).

8. Fix the sugarpaste flowers around the cake-base.

11. Decorate inscription with piped lines and dots (No. 1).

9. Pipe inscription of choice on cake-top (No. 1).

12. Fix teddy bear to cake-top in the position shown.

WORK NOTES

13. Fix further flowers and then pipe grass (No. 1) around the teddy bear.

14. Fix candles and holders on cake-top, as required.

COST SUMMARY

DATE _____ NAME _____ BOOK _____
PAGE _____ SIZE _____ SHAPE _____
CAKE _____ COVERING _____ COATING _____

A PRODUCTS	Used	Cost
_____	_____	_____
_____	_____	_____
_____	_____	_____
_____	_____	_____
_____	_____	_____
_____	_____	_____
_____	_____	_____
_____	_____	_____
_____	_____	_____
_____	_____	_____
_____	_____	_____
_____	_____	_____
_____	_____	_____
_____	_____	_____
_____	_____	_____
_____	_____	_____
_____	_____	_____

Subtotal: **A** = £ _____

B TIME TAKEN — Minutes

Total _____
Charge per minute × p
Total _____
LABOUR CHARGE Subtotal **B** = £ _____

Subtotals **A** + **B** = TOTAL COST = £ _____
OVERHEAD COSTS = £ _____
PROFIT COSTS = £ _____
GRAND TOTAL = £ _____

NOTE: Please refer to the information on pages 5–10 before attempting to complete this COST SHEET.
A 'MASTER' Cost Sheet can be found on page 116.

Luke

LUKE'S CAKE PROFILE
OCCASION – BIRTHDAY

CAKE	–	GENOESE SPONGE			PAGE 13
SHAPE	–	FIGURE 6	25.5cm	10in	
BOARD	–	ROUND	33cm	13in	
FILLING	–	BUTTERCREAM	115g	4oz	PAGE 19
COVERING	–	BUTTERCREAM	115g	4oz	PAGE 19
COATING	–	SUGARPASTE	570g	1lb 4oz	PAGE 17
PIPING	–	ROYAL ICING	340g	12oz	PAGE 19

WORK NOTES

DECORATING THE CAKE
STEPS 2–8

TIME

STARTED   _____

FINISHED   _____

TIME TAKEN   _____

1. Picture showing coated cake on doyley and board.

DECORATING THE CAKE
2. Fix ribbon around cake-side. Roll out, cut and fix a sugarpaste disc to cake-top.

3. Pipe shells around cake-base and the part of the cake-top edge shown (No. 7).

4. Pipe scrolls around the remainder of the cake-top edge (No. 7).

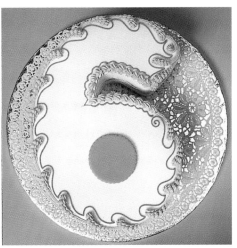

5. Pipe a line beside each cake-top scroll and shell (No. 2).

6. Overpipe each scroll (No. 2).

WORK NOTES

7. Pipe inscription of choice on cake-top (No. 1).

8. Fix decorations of choice to cake-top and board.

COST SUMMARY

DATE _____ NAME _____ BOOK _____
PAGE _____ SIZE _____ SHAPE _____
CAKE _____ COVERING _____ COATING _____

A PRODUCTS	Used	Cost
	Subtotal: **A** = £ _____	

B TIME TAKEN — Minutes

Total _____
Charge per minute × p
Total _____
LABOUR CHARGE Subtotal **B** = £ _____

Subtotals **A** + **B** = TOTAL COST = £ _____
OVERHEAD COSTS = £ _____
PROFIT COSTS = £ _____
GRAND TOTAL = £ _____

NOTE: Please refer to the information on pages 5–10 before attempting to complete this COST SHEET.
A 'MASTER' Cost Sheet can be found on page 116.

Miranda

MIRANDA'S CAKE PROFILE
OCCASION – ANNIVERSARY

CAKE	– FRUIT CAKE			PAGE 16
SHAPE	– ROUND	20.5cm	8in	
BOARD	– ROUND	30.5cm	12in	
COVERING	– ALMOND PASTE	455g	16oz	PAGE 17
COATING	– SUGARPASTE	905g	2lb	PAGE 17
PIPING	– ROYAL ICING	225g	8oz	PAGE 19

61

Miranda

WORK NOTES

DECORATING THE CAKE
STEPS 2–14

TIME

STARTED   _____

FINISHED   _____

TIME TAKEN   _____

1. Picture showing coated cake on coated board (with crimped edge).

DECORATING THE CAKE
2. Pipe shells (No. 2) around the cake-base.

3. Roll out and cut a disc of sugarpaste (to cover cake-top and side as shown). Flute the disc edge by rolling a cocktail stick backwards and forwards a little at a time. Immediately fix the sugarpaste in the position shown. Leave to dry for 24 hours.

4. Lay a plastic doyley on the cake-top, as shown.

5. Spread a thin layer of royal icing over the doyley using a trowel shaped palette knife.

6. Immediately peel off the doyley in one continuous movement.

62

7. Pipe curved lines beside doyley pattern (No. 1).

10. Roll out, cut and shape three sizes of sugarpaste flower heads. Make as many as required to suit the design chosen.

8. Pipe series of dots beside the curved lines, as shown (No. 1).

11. Pipe a ring of dots on each flower, as shown (No. 1).

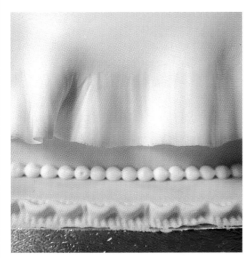

9. Brush edge of fluted disc with edible confectioners' dusting powder.

12. Fix the flowers to the cake as shown.

WORK NOTES

13. Pipe graduated dots beside each cake-side flower (No. 1).

14. Make and fix a sugarpaste central display and add artificial decorations of choice.

COST SUMMARY

DATE _____ NAME _____ BOOK _____
PAGE _____ SIZE _____ SHAPE _____
CAKE _____ COVERING _____ COATING _____

A PRODUCTS	Used	Cost
		Subtotal: **A** = £ _____

B TIME TAKEN	Minutes
Total	_____
Charge per minute	× p
Total	_____
LABOUR CHARGE Subtotal **B** =	£ _____

Subtotals **A** + **B** = TOTAL COST = £ _____
OVERHEAD COSTS = £ _____
PROFIT COSTS = £ _____
GRAND TOTAL = £ _____

NOTE: Please refer to the information on pages 5–10 before attempting to complete this COST SHEET.
A 'MASTER' Cost Sheet can be found on page 116.

Flora

FLORA'S CAKE PROFILE
OCCASION – WEDDING

CAKE	–	FRUIT CAKE			PAGE 16
SHAPE	–	SQUARE	20.5cm	8in	
BOARD	–	SQUARE	28cm	11in	
BOARD	–	SQUARE	30.5cm	12in	
COVERING	–	ALMOND PASTE	905g	2lb	PAGE 17
COATING	–	SUGARPASTE	905g	2lb	PAGE 17
PIPING	–	ROYAL ICING	340g	12oz	PAGE 19

Flora

WORK NOTES

CRYSTALLISED FLOWERS
STEPS 1–3

TIME

STARTED   _____

FINISHED   _____

TIME TAKEN   _____

DECORATING THE CAKE
STEPS 4–14

TIME

STARTED   _____

FINISHED   _____

TIME TAKEN   _____

CRYSTALLISED FLOWERS

1. Mix together 2 teaspoons of cold water with 1 egg white. Brush the top surface of a freshly picked primrose with this solution.

4. Picture showing a square cake on two cake-boards and covered with sugarpaste.

2. Immediately sprinkle caster sugar on to the flower. Upturn flower and gently shake off the surplus sugar.

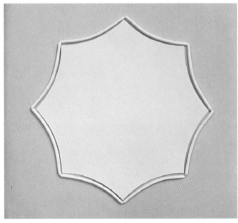

DECORATING THE CAKE

5. Cut and place a 18cm (7in) wide paper template on cake-top in the shape shown. Pipe lines beside the template (No. 3).

3. Repeat step 2 on the underside of the flower, and then place on greaseproof paper. Leave to crystallise for 24 hours. 12 crystallised primrose heads and 8 crystallised sprigs of rosemary are required.

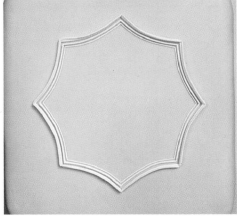

6. Carefully remove the template. Overpipe the No. 3 line (No. 2), then pipe beside and overpipe the No. 2 line (No. 1).

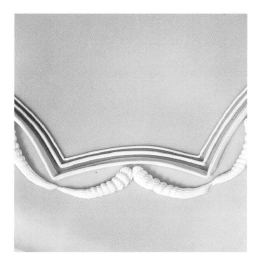

7. Pipe 'C' scrolls (No. 42) beside the piped lines, as shown.

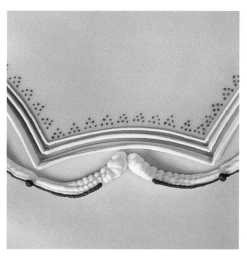

10. Overpipe each scroll (No. 1). Pipe dots on cake-top as shown (No. 1).

8. Fix ribbon to each cake-board edge. Pipe shells around cake-base (No. 2), then pipe shells around board edge (No. 42).

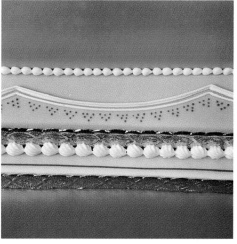

11. Pipe dots beside the cake-board piped lines (No. 1). Pipe a line on the bottom board (No. 1).

9. Overpipe each scroll (No. 2). Pipe curved lines on cake board, as shown (No. 2). Then pipe beside and overpipe the No. 2 lines (No. 1).

12. Fix ribbons around cake side. Make and fix a ribbon loop to each cake-base corner.

WORK NOTES

13. Fix the crystallised primroses and rosemary sprigs to cake-top corners and board, as shown.

14. Fix artificial decorations of choice, to cake-top centre.

COST SUMMARY

DATE _____ NAME _____ BOOK _____

PAGE _____ SIZE _____ SHAPE _____

CAKE _____ COVERING _____ COATING _____

A PRODUCTS	Used	Cost
	Subtotal: **A** = £ _____

B TIME TAKEN	Minutes
Total	_____
Charge per minute	× ____ p
Total	_____
LABOUR CHARGE Subtotal **B** =	£ _____

Subtotals **A** + **B** = TOTAL COST = £ _____

OVERHEAD COSTS = £ _____

PROFIT COSTS = £ _____

GRAND TOTAL = £ _____

NOTE: Please refer to the information on pages 5–10 before attempting to complete this COST SHEET.
A 'MASTER' Cost Sheet can be found on page 116.

Carla

CARLA'S CAKE PROFILE
OCCASION – CHRISTENING

CAKE	–	FRUIT CAKE			PAGE 16
SHAPE	–	ROUND	20.5cm	8in	
BOARD	–	ROUND	28cm	11in	
COVERING	–	ALMOND PASTE	680g	1lb 8oz	PAGE 17
COATING	–	ROYAL ICING	455g	16oz	PAGE 19
PIPING	–	ROYAL ICING	340g	12oz	PAGE 19

Carla

WORK NOTES

MAKING CRADLE
STEP 1

TIME

STARTED   _____

FINISHED   _____

TIME TAKEN   _____

MAKING SWANS
STEP 2

TIME

STARTED   _____

FINISHED   _____

TIME TAKEN   _____

DECORATING CRADLE
AND SWANS
STEPS 3–5

TIME

STARTED   _____

FINISHED   _____

TIME TAKEN   _____

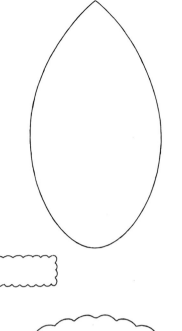

CRADLE TEMPLATES

SWAN TEMPLATES

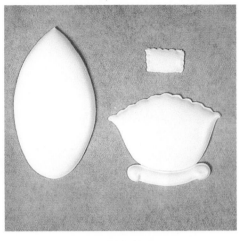

MAKING CRADLE

1. Outline (No. 1) and flood-in on waxed paper, each of the cradle template shapes shown. Leave to dry for 24 hours.

MAKING SWANS

2. Outline (No. 1) and flood-in on waxed paper, each of the swan template shapes shown. Leave to dry for 24 hours.

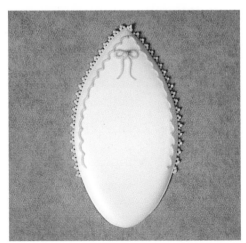

DECORATING CRADLE AND SWANS

3. Decorate the cradle head with piped royal icing, as shown (No. 0). Leave to dry for 2 hours.

WORK NOTES

DECORATING THE CAKE
STEPS 6–11

TIME

STARTED ————————

FINISHED ————————

TIME TAKEN ————————

4. Decorate the cradle pillow and front, as shown (No. 1). Leave to dry for 2 hours.

7. Fix ribbon loops to each swan, then pipe a line from each beak to each cradle side (No. 1).

5. Paint the swans' eyes and beaks with edible food colouring. Leave to dry for 2 hours.

8. Pipe scrolls and shells around the cake-top edge as shown (No. 43).

DECORATING THE CAKE

6. Fix cradle parts and swans in the positions shown on the coated cake.

9. Pipe shells around the cake base (No. 43).

71

WORK NOTES

10. Pipe curved lines beside the cake-top scrolls (No. 2).

11. Overpipe each scroll (No. 2). Decorate the cake with ribbons and artificial flowers of choice.

COST SUMMARY

DATE _____ NAME _____ BOOK _____
PAGE _____ SIZE _____ SHAPE _____
CAKE _____ COVERING _____ COATING _____

A PRODUCTS	Used	Cost
	Subtotal: **A** = £ _____	

B TIME TAKEN   Minutes

Total _____
Charge per minute   ×   p
Total _____
LABOUR CHARGE   Subtotal **B** = £ _____

Subtotals **A** + **B** = TOTAL COST = £ _____
OVERHEAD COSTS = £ _____
PROFIT COSTS = £ _____
GRAND TOTAL = £ _____

NOTE: Please refer to the information on pages 5–10 before attempting to complete this COST SHEET.
A 'MASTER' Cost Sheet can be found on page 116.

DONNA'S CAKE PROFILE
OCCASION – WEDDING

CAKE	– FRUIT CAKE			PAGE 16
SHAPE	– HEART	25.5cm	10in	
BOARD	– ROUND	35.5cm	14in	
COVERING	– ALMOND PASTE	1Kg	2lb 3oz	PAGE 17
COATING	– ROYAL ICING	795g	1lb 12oz	PAGE 19
PIPING	– ROYAL ICING	340g	12oz	PAGE 19

WORK NOTES

MAKING THE
MONOGRAM
STEP 1

TIME

STARTED   _____

FINISHED   _____

TIME TAKEN   _____

DECORATING THE
MONOGRAM
STEP 2

TIME

STARTED   _____

FINISHED   _____

TIME TAKEN   _____

DECORATING THE CAKE
STEPS 5–13

TIME

STARTED   _____

FINISHED   _____

TIME TAKEN   _____

MONOGRAM MODEL

3. The Mary Ford cake scraper shown (or scraper cut to this shape) is required.

MAKING THE MONOGRAM
1. Outline (No. 1) and flood-in on waxed paper the chosen monogram, using the model as a guide. Leave to dry for 24 hours.

4. A cake coated in royal icing (using scraper illustrated, for cake-side final coat) is required.

DECORATING THE MONOGRAM
2. Pipe dots around the runout edge (No. 0). Leave to dry for 2 hours.

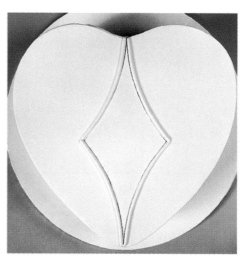

DECORATING THE CAKE
5. Make a paper template in the shape shown and place on cake-top. Pipe a line beside the template (No. 4).

6. Pipe bulbs against the cake-top curved lines, as shown (No. 3).

9. Pipe bulbs around the cake-base (No. 3) then pipe a line over each bulb (No. 2), then overpipe the No. 2 line (No. 1). Pipe dots, as shown (No. 1).

7. Pipe filigree inside the cake-top design (No. 0).

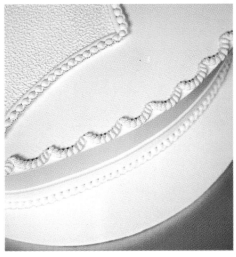

10. Pipe curved rope design around cake-top edge (No. 43).

8. Pipe a line over each bulb (No. 2), then overpipe the No. 2 line (No. 1). Pipe dots, as shown (No. 1).

11. Pipe curved rope design around cake-board edge (No. 43).

WORK NOTES

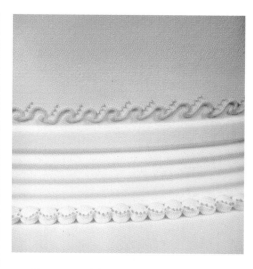

12. Pipe curved lines and dots on the cake-side, as shown (No. 1).

13. Pipe graduated dots beside each rope design (No. 1). Fix monogram, decorations and ribbons of choice to the cake.

COST SUMMARY

DATE _____ NAME _____ BOOK _____
PAGE _____ SIZE _____ SHAPE _____
CAKE _____ COVERING _____ COATING _____

A PRODUCTS	Used	Cost	**B TIME TAKEN**	Minutes
_____	_____	_____	_____	_____
_____	_____	_____	_____	_____
_____	_____	_____	_____	_____
_____	_____	_____	_____	_____
_____	_____	_____	_____	_____
_____	_____	_____	_____	_____
_____	_____	_____	_____	_____
_____	_____	_____	_____	_____

Total _____

Charge per minute × p

Total _____

LABOUR CHARGE Subtotal **B** = £ _____

Subtotals **A** + **B** = TOTAL COST = £ _____
OVERHEAD COSTS = £ _____
PROFIT COSTS = £ _____
GRAND TOTAL = £ _____

Subtotal: **A** = £ _____

NOTE: Please refer to the information on pages 5–10 before attempting to complete this COST SHEET.
A 'MASTER' Cost Sheet can be found on page 116.

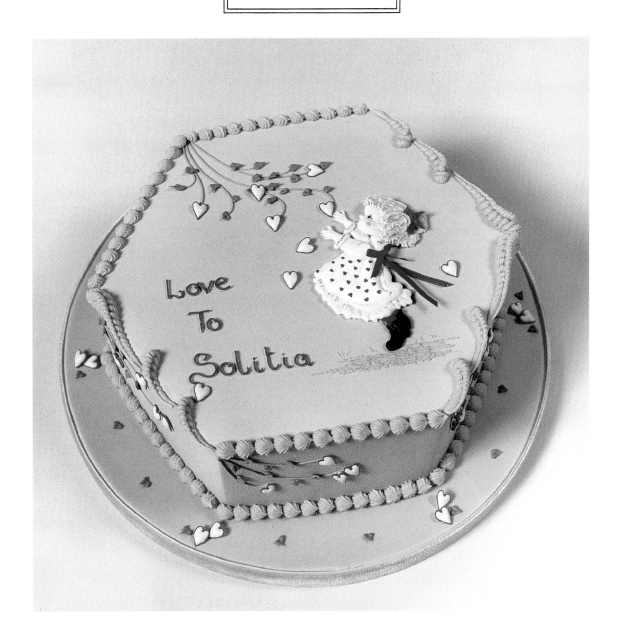

SOLITIA'S CAKE PROFILE
OCCASION – BIRTHDAY

CAKE	–	FRUIT CAKE			PAGE 16
SHAPE	–	HEXAGONAL	20.5cm	8in	
BOARD	–	ROUND	30.5cm	12in	
COVERING	–	ALMOND PASTE	680g	1lb 8oz	PAGE 17
COATING	–	ROYAL ICING	455g	16oz	PAGE 19
PIPING	–	ROYAL ICING	340g	12oz	PAGE 19

WORK NOTES

MAKING RUNOUT FIGURE
STEPS 1–3

TIME

STARTED   ————

FINISHED   ————

TIME TAKEN   ————

DECORATING THE FIGURE
STEP 4

TIME

STARTED   ————

FINISHED   ————

TIME TAKEN   ————

HEART
TEMPLATE

SOLITIA'S TEMPLATE

2. Pipe-in the further parts shown.

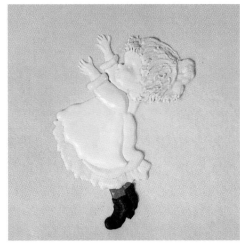

3. Pipe-in remaining parts shown. Leave to dry for 24 hours.

MAKING RUNOUT FIGURE
1. Trace Solitia's template on to card, cover with waxed paper and pipe-in the parts shown with royal icing.

DECORATING THE FIGURE
4. Pipe hearts on the dress (No. 0), then paint the figure with edible food colouring.

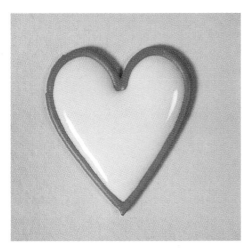

MAKING RUNOUT HEARTS
5. Picture showing enlarged runout heart. Outline (No. 1) and flood-in 36 hearts on waxed paper (using heart template as guide). Leave to dry for 24 hours.

8. Fix the runout figure and hearts to cake, as shown.

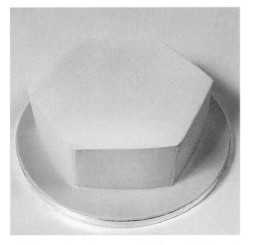

6. Picture showing coated cake on its board.

9. Pipe grass and inscription of choice on cake-top (No. 1).

DECORATING THE CAKE
7. Pipe curved lines on cake-top and sides (No. 2) to form branches. Pipe leaves on each branch, as shown.

10. Pipe scrolls and shells around the cake-top edge and base, as shown (No. 43).

WORK NOTES

MAKING RUNOUT HEARTS
STEP 5

TIME

STARTED   ———————

FINISHED   ———————

TIME TAKEN   ———————

DECORATING THE CAKE
STEPS 7–12

TIME

STARTED   ———————

FINISHED   ———————

TIME TAKEN   ———————

WORK NOTES

11. Overpipe each scroll (No. 2).

12. Pipe leaves on the cake-board. Then fix runout hearts at each cake-base corner.

COST SUMMARY

DATE _____ NAME _____ BOOK _____

PAGE _____ SIZE _____ SHAPE _____

CAKE _____ COVERING _____ COATING _____

A PRODUCTS	Used	Cost
	Subtotal: **A** = £ _____	

B TIME TAKEN	Minutes
Total	_____
Charge per minute	× p
Total	_____
LABOUR CHARGE	Subtotal **B** = £ _____

Subtotals **A** + **B** = TOTAL COST =	£ _____
OVERHEAD COSTS =	£ _____
PROFIT COSTS =	£ _____
GRAND TOTAL =	£ _____

NOTE: Please refer to the information on pages 5–10 before attempting to complete this COST SHEET.
A 'MASTER' Cost Sheet can be found on page 116.

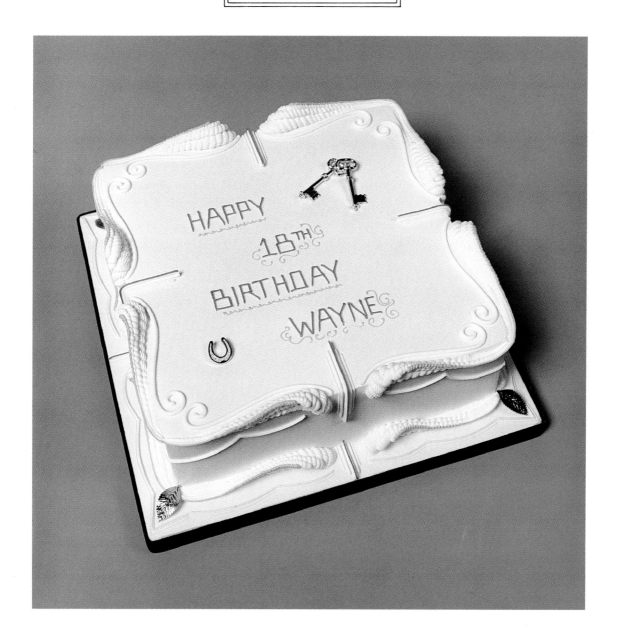

WAYNE'S CAKE PROFILE
OCCASION – BIRTHDAY

CAKE	–	FRUIT CAKE			PAGE 16
SHAPE	–	SQUARE	20.5cm	8in	
BOARD	–	SQUARE	28cm	11in	
COVERING	–	ALMOND PASTE	905g	2lb	PAGE 17
COATING	–	ROYAL ICING	680g	1lb 8oz	PAGE 19
PIPING	–	ROYAL ICING	170g	6oz	PAGE 19

WORK NOTES

DECORATING THE CAKE
STEPS 1–14

TIME

STARTED   _____

FINISHED   _____

TIME TAKEN   _____

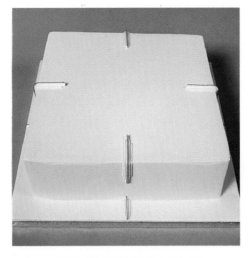

DECORATING THE CAKE

1. Pipe graduated lines on the cake-top edge and board as shown (Nos.3,2,1).

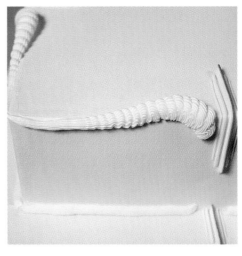

4. Pipe a right-to-left scroll on the cake-top edge, as shown (No. 44).

2. Pipe a thick line around each cake-base corner (No. 44).

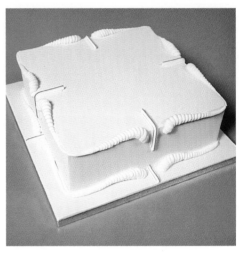

5. Pipe matching scrolls around the cake-top edge and base (No. 44).

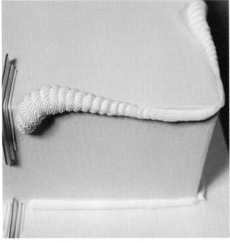

3. Pipe a left-to-right scroll on the cake-top edge, as shown (No. 44).

6. Pipe a curved line beside each cake-top scroll (No. 3).

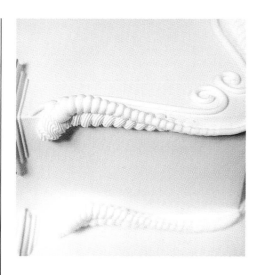

7. Overpipe each scroll (No. 3).

10. Pipe lines on the cake-board corners, as shown (No. 2).

8. Pipe curved lines against each cake-side, as shown (No. 2).

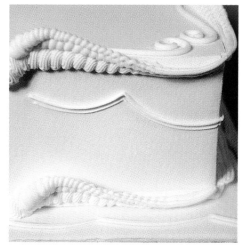

11. Pipe a line below and then against each cake-side piped line (No. 1).

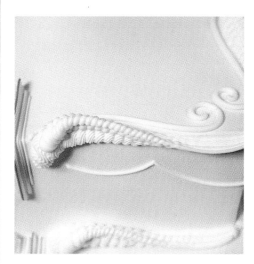

9. Overpipe each scroll (No. 2).

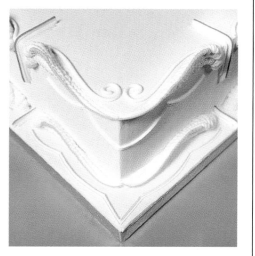

12. Overpipe each scroll (No. 1).

WORK NOTES

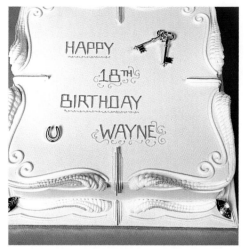

13. Pipe and decorate inscription of choice on the cake-top (No. 1).

14. Fix decorations of choice to the cake-top and cake-board corners. Fix ribbon around cake-board edge.

COST SUMMARY		

DATE _____ NAME _____ BOOK _____
PAGE _____ SIZE _____ SHAPE _____
CAKE _____ COVERING _____ COATING _____

A PRODUCTS	Used	Cost
_____	_____	_____
_____	_____	_____
_____	_____	_____
_____	_____	_____
_____	_____	_____
_____	_____	_____
_____	_____	_____
_____	_____	_____
_____	_____	_____
_____	_____	_____
_____	_____	_____
_____	_____	_____
_____	_____	_____
_____	_____	_____
_____	_____	_____
	Subtotal: **A** = £ _____

B TIME TAKEN	Minutes
_____	_____
_____	_____
_____	_____
_____	_____
_____	_____
_____	_____
_____	_____
_____	_____
Total	_____
Charge per minute	× p
Total	_____
LABOUR CHARGE	Subtotal **B** = £ _____

Subtotals **A** + **B** = TOTAL COST = £ _____
OVERHEAD COSTS = £ _____
PROFIT COSTS = £ _____
GRAND TOTAL = £ _____

NOTE: Please refer to the information on pages 5–10 before attempting to complete this COST SHEET.
A 'MASTER' Cost Sheet can be found on page 116.

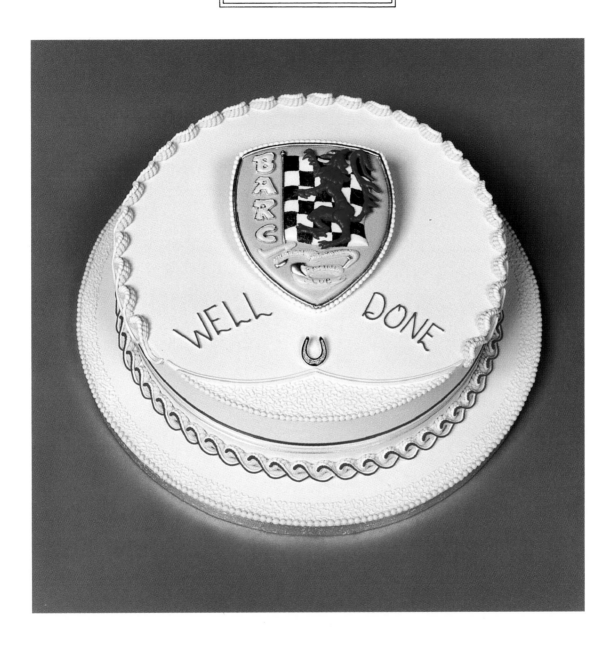

STEVEN'S CAKE PROFILE
OCCASION – CELEBRATION

CAKE	– FRUIT CAKE			PAGE 16
SHAPE	– ROUND	23cm	9in	
BOARD	– ROUND	30.5cm	12in	
COVERING	– ALMOND PASTE	905g	2lb	PAGE 17
COATING	– ROYAL ICING	570g	1lb 4oz	PAGE 19
PIPING	– ROYAL ICING	455g	16oz	PAGE 19

STEVEN'S TEMPLATES

MAKING THE SHIELD RUNOUTS

1. Outline (No. 1) and flood-in the shield on waxed paper (using template as guide). Leave to dry for 24 hours.

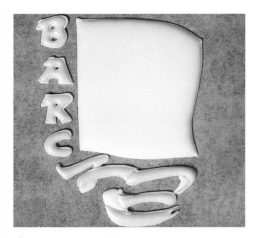

WORK NOTES

DECORATING THE SHIELD
STEPS 4–6

TIME

STARTED   —————

FINISHED   —————

TIME TAKEN —————

2. Outline (No. 0) and flood-in the flag, letters and ribbon on waxed paper (using the templates as guides).

5. Pipe the flag staff (No. 2). Then pipe names on the ribbon and a line around each letter (No. 0). Leave to dry for 1 hour. Paint the parts shown with edible food colouring.

3. Pipe-in the lion on waxed paper (using template as guide). Leave to dry for 24 hours.

6. Fix runout pieces to the shield in the positions shown.

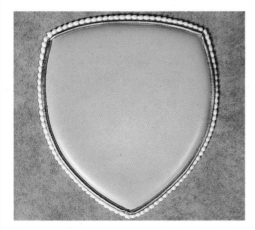

DECORATING THE SHIELD

4. Pipe a line against the shield edge (No. 3). Leave to dry for 3 hours. Then paint the line with edible food colouring. Pipe shells against the piped line (No. 2). Leave to dry for 12 hours.

7. Picture showing the coated cake and board.

WORK NOTES

DECORATING THE CAKE
STEPS 8–15

TIME

STARTED _____

FINISHED _____

TIME TAKEN _____

DECORATING THE CAKE
8. Cut and fix a sugarpaste wedge to cake-top centre. Pipe shells around wedge base (No. 2).

11. Pipe the curved lines, as shown (Nos.2,1). Pipe filigree between the lines and cake edge (No. 0). Pipe shells along cake-top edge (No. 2). Pipe a line around the cake-base (No. 43).

9. Fix badge to wedge, as shown.

12. Pipe scrolls around cake-top edge and base, as shown (No. 43).

10. Pipe inscription of choice to cake-top (No. 1). Fix decoration of choice in the position shown.

13. Overpipe each scroll (No. 2).

14. Overpipe each cake-base scroll (No. 1).

15. Pipe filigree around top edge of cake-board (No. 1). Pipe shells around cake-board edge (No. 2). Fix ribbons to cake-side.

COST SUMMARY

DATE _____ NAME _____ BOOK _____

PAGE _____ SIZE _____ SHAPE _____

CAKE _____ COVERING _____ COATING _____

A PRODUCTS	Used	Cost
	Subtotal: **A** = £ _____	

B TIME TAKEN	Minutes
Total	_____
Charge per minute	× p
Total	_____
LABOUR CHARGE	Subtotal **B** = £ _____
Subtotals **A** + **B** = TOTAL COST =	£ _____
OVERHEAD COSTS =	£ _____
PROFIT COSTS =	£ _____
GRAND TOTAL =	£ _____

NOTE: Please refer to the information on pages 5–10 before attempting to complete this COST SHEET.
A 'MASTER' Cost Sheet can be found on page 116.

CATHIE'S CAKE PROFILE
OCCASION – WEDDING

CAKE	–	FRUIT CAKE			PAGE 16
SHAPE	–	HEXAGONAL	15/23cm	6/9in	
BOARD	–	ROUND	23/33cm	9/13in	
COVERING	–	ALMOND PASTE	905g	2lb	PAGE 17
COATING	–	SUGARPASTE	905g	2lb	PAGE 17
PIPING	–	ROYAL ICING	455g	16oz	PAGE 19

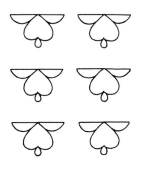

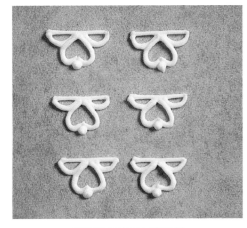

CATHIE'S TEMPLATES

PIPED LINE MOTIFS

3. Pipe the line motifs shown (No. 1) on waxed paper (using template as guide). Leave to dry for 24 hours. 80 motifs are required.

MAKING THE RUNOUT
BORDER
STEP 2

TIME

STARTED   ———

FINISHED   ———

TIME TAKEN   ———

PIPED LINE MOTIFS
STEP 3

TIME

STARTED   ———

FINISHED   ———

TIME TAKEN   ———

PIPED FLOWERS
STEPS 4–8

TIME

STARTED   ———

FINISHED   ———

TIME TAKEN   ———

1. Picture showing coated cakes on their boards.

PIPED FLOWERS

4. Fill a piping bag with royal icing in two colours. Pipe a petal on waxed paper (No. 57).

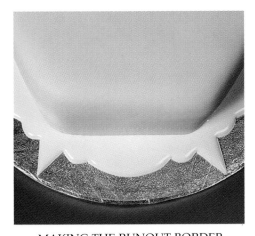

MAKING THE RUNOUT BORDER

2. Outline on each cake-board the design shown (No. 2). Flood-in between each outline and cake-base. Leave to dry for 24 hours.

5. Pipe the second petal, as shown (No. 57).

6. Pipe the third and fourth petals, as shown (No. 57).

DECORATING THE CAKE

9. Pipe shells around the base of each cake (No. 2).

7. Pipe the fifth petal to complete the flower shape (No. 57). Leave to dry for 2 hours. 70 flowers are required.

10. Fix motifs to each cake-side in design shown.

8. Pipe a dot in the centre of each flower (No. 2). Leave to dry for 24 hours.

11. Pipe the design shown (No. 1) on each cake-top edge.

12. Fix a piped sugar flower to each cake-top corner.

13. Fix artificial horseshoes and piped sugar flowers around cake-base, as shown.

COST SUMMARY

DATE _____ NAME _____ BOOK _____
PAGE _____ SIZE _____ SHAPE _____
CAKE _____ COVERING _____ COATING _____

A PRODUCTS	Used	Cost
_____	_____	_____
_____	_____	_____
_____	_____	_____
_____	_____	_____
_____	_____	_____
_____	_____	_____
_____	_____	_____
_____	_____	_____
_____	_____	_____
_____	_____	_____
_____	_____	_____
_____	_____	_____
_____	_____	_____
_____	_____	_____
_____	_____	_____
_____	_____	_____
_____	_____	_____
_____	_____	_____
	Subtotal: **A** =	£ _____

B TIME TAKEN	Minutes
_____	_____
_____	_____
_____	_____
_____	_____
_____	_____
_____	_____
_____	_____
_____	_____
_____	_____
Total	_____
Charge per minute	× p
Total	_____
LABOUR CHARGE Subtotal **B** =	£ _____

Subtotals **A** + **B** = TOTAL COST =	£ _____
OVERHEAD COSTS =	£ _____
PROFIT COSTS =	£ _____
GRAND TOTAL =	£ _____

NOTE: Please refer to the information on pages 5–10 before attempting to complete this COST SHEET.
A 'MASTER' Cost Sheet can be found on page 116.

Aileen

AILEEN'S CAKE PROFILE
OCCASION – WEDDING

CAKE	– FRUIT CAKE			PAGE 16
SHAPE	– SQUARE	15/20.5/25.5cm	6/8/10in	
BOARD	– SQUARE	20.5/25.5/35cm	8/10/14in	
COVERING	– ALMOND PASTE	2.7Kg	6lb	PAGE 17
COATING	– ROYAL ICING	1.4Kg	3lb	PAGE 19
PIPING	– ROYAL ICING	1.4Kg	3lb	PAGE 19

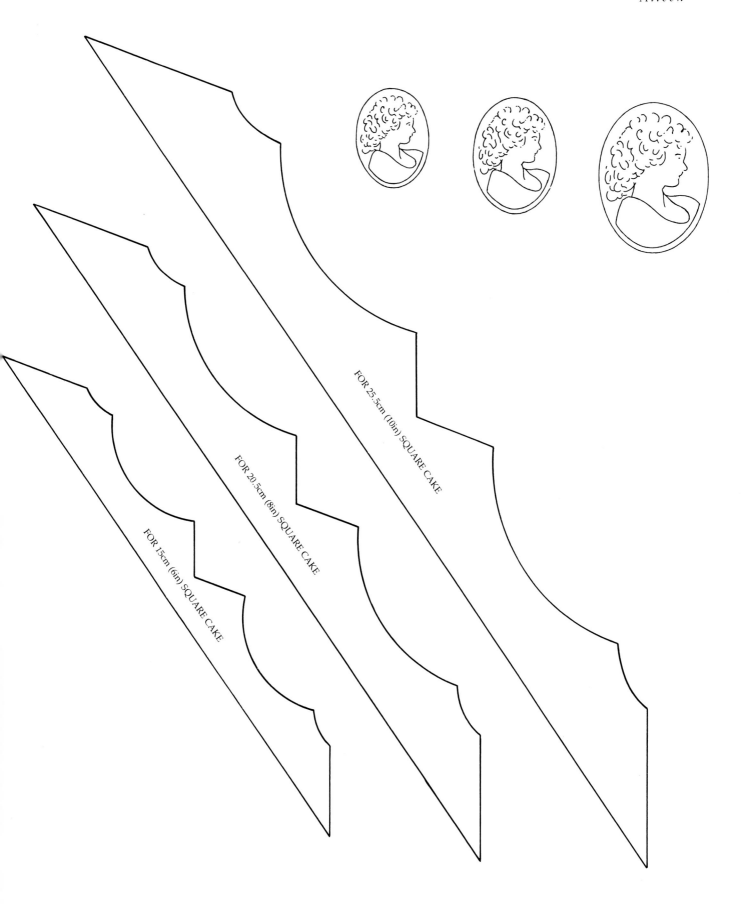

FOR 25.5cm (10in) SQUARE CAKE

FOR 20.5cm (8in) SQUARE CAKE

FOR 15cm (6in) SQUARE CAKE

AILEEN'S TEMPLATES

WORK NOTES

MAKING THE PLAQUES
STEP 1

TIME

STARTED   _____

FINISHED   _____

TIME TAKEN   _____

MAKING THE FIGURES
STEP 2

TIME

STARTED   _____

FINISHED   _____

TIME TAKEN   _____

FINISHING THE PLAQUES
STEPS 3–4

TIME

STARTED   _____

FINISHED   _____

TIME TAKEN   _____

CAKE RUNOUT
STEPS 6–7

TIME

STARTED   _____

FINISHED   _____

TIME TAKEN   _____

MAKING THE PLAQUES
1. Outline and flood-in 4 plaques of each size on waxed paper (using templates as a guide) (No. 1). Leave to dry for 24 hours.

MAKING THE FIGURES
2. Pipe-in 4 figures of each size, on waxed paper (using templates as a guide). Leave to dry for 24 hours.

FINISHING THE PLAQUES
3. Pipe shells around the edge of each plaque, as shown (No. 1).

4. Fix a figure to each plaque. Leave to dry for 2 hours.

5. Picture showing three coated cakes on their respective boards.

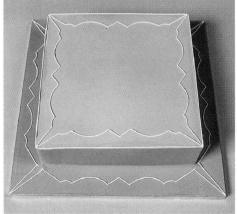

CAKE RUNOUT
6. Pipe an outline on each cake-top and board, as shown, using the relevant template as a guide (No. 2).

WORK NOTES

DECORATING THE CAKE
STEPS 8–14

TIME

STARTED   ———

FINISHED   ———

TIME TAKEN   ———

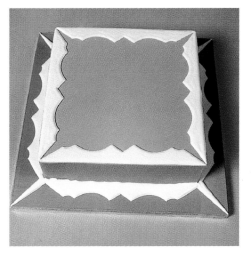

7. Flood-in the design, using softened royal icing – without glycerine. Leave to dry for 24 hours.

10. Pipe a line beside the cake-base runout (No. 2). Then pipe a line beside and overpipe the No. 2 line (No. 1).

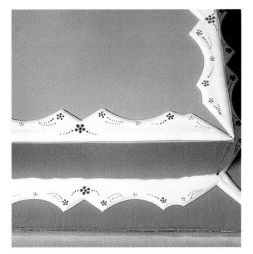

DECORATING THE CAKE
8. Pipe floral motifs on runout borders, as shown (No. 1).

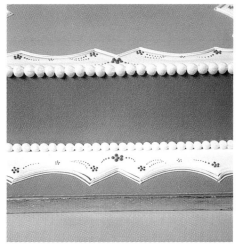

11. Pipe shells around the cake-top edge and base (No. 3).

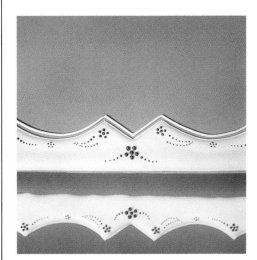

9. Pipe a line beside each cake-top runout (No. 2).

12. Pipe a line over each shell, as shown (No. 1).

WORK NOTES

13. Fix a plaque to each cake-side.

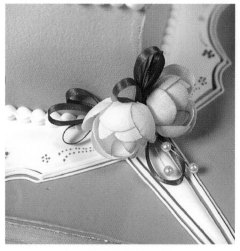

14. Fix artificial flowers, ribbon loops and pearls to each cake-base corner. Fix ribbon around each cake-board edge.

COST SUMMARY

DATE _____ NAME _____ BOOK _____
PAGE _____ SIZE _____ SHAPE _____
CAKE _____ COVERING _____ COATING _____

A PRODUCTS	Used	Cost
_____	_____	_____
_____	_____	_____
_____	_____	_____
_____	_____	_____
_____	_____	_____
_____	_____	_____
_____	_____	_____
_____	_____	_____
_____	_____	_____
_____	_____	_____
_____	_____	_____
_____	_____	_____
_____	_____	_____
_____	_____	_____
_____	_____	_____
_____	_____	_____

Subtotal: **A** = £ _____

B TIME TAKEN	Minutes
_____	_____
_____	_____
_____	_____
_____	_____
_____	_____
_____	_____
_____	_____
_____	_____
_____	_____

Total _____

Charge per minute × p

Total _____

LABOUR CHARGE Subtotal **B** = £ _____

Subtotals **A** + **B** = TOTAL COST = £ _____

OVERHEAD COSTS = £ _____

PROFIT COSTS = £ _____

GRAND TOTAL = £ _____

NOTE: Please refer to the information on pages 5–10 before attempting to complete this COST SHEET.
A 'MASTER' Cost Sheet can be found on page 116.

HENRIETTA'S CAKE PROFILE
OCCASION – WEDDING

CAKE	– FRUIT CAKE			PAGE 16
SHAPE	– ROUND	15/23cm	6/9in	
TOP BOARD	– ROUND	23cm	9in	
BASE BOARDS	– ROUND	30.5/33cm	12/13in	
COVERING	– ALMOND PASTE	1.4Kg	3lb	PAGE 17
COATING	– ROYAL ICING	905g	2lb	PAGE 19
PIPING	– ROYAL ICING	455g	16oz	PAGE 19

Henrietta

WORK NOTES

DECORATING THE CAKE
STEPS 2–14

TIME

STARTED _____

FINISHED _____

TIME TAKEN _____

1. Picture showing coated cakes on their respective boards.

4. Pipe a line between each cake-base lattice design (No. 43). Pipe scrolls on the cake-top edge and base, as shown (No. 43).

DECORATING THE CAKE

2. Divide each cake-top edge into 12 equal portions. Pipe a series of lines, to form lattice, on every third portion (No. 1).

5. Overpipe each scroll (No. 3).

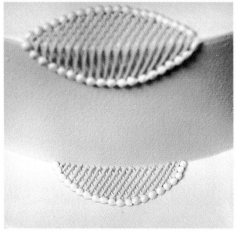

3. Repeat at cake-base, in the shape shown (No. 1). Then pipe shells around the lattice edges (No. 2).

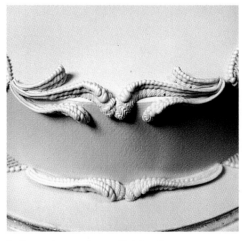

6. Overpipe each scroll (No. 2).

7. Pipe curved lines against each cake-side, as shown (No. 2).

10. Pipe a line beside and overpipe each No. 2 line (No. 1).

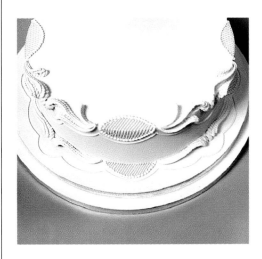

8. Pipe curved lines on the cake-board top, beside the cake-base design (No. 2).

11. Pipe a scalloped line beside each of the curved lines, as indicated (No. 0).

9. Overpipe each scroll (No. 1).

12. Fix paper band around each cake-board edge and then pipe shells on the bottom tier board, as shown (No. 2).

WORK NOTES

13. Pipe a line on each shell (No. 1). Then pipe a scalloped line on the cake-board edge (No. 1).

14. Decorate each cake with artificial flowers and leaves.

COST SUMMARY

DATE _____ NAME _____ BOOK _____

PAGE _____ SIZE _____ SHAPE _____

CAKE _____ COVERING _____ COATING _____

A PRODUCTS	Used	Cost	**B** TIME TAKEN	Minutes

Total	_____
Charge per minute	× p
Total	_____
LABOUR CHARGE	Subtotal **B** = £ _____

Subtotal: **A** = £ _____

Subtotals **A** + **B** = TOTAL COST =	£ _____
OVERHEAD COSTS =	£ _____
PROFIT COSTS =	£ _____
GRAND TOTAL =	£ _____

NOTE: Please refer to the information on pages 5–10 before attempting to complete this COST SHEET. A 'MASTER' Cost Sheet can be found on page 116.

Bella

BELLA'S CAKE PROFILE
OCCASION – CHRISTMAS

CAKE	– FRUIT CAKE			PAGE 16
SHAPE	– SQUARE	20.5cm	8in	
BOARD	– SQUARE	28cm	11in	
COVERING	– ALMOND PASTE	680g	1lb 8oz	PAGE 17
COATING	– SUGARPASTE	680g	1lb 8oz	PAGE 17
PIPING	– ROYAL ICING	340g	12oz	PAGE 19

BELLA'S TEMPLATES

MAKING THE POINSETTIA

3. Pipe the leaves on waxed paper (using template as a guide) (No. 2). Leave to dry for 2 hours. 8 poinsettias are required.

1. Picture showing coated cake and board (with crimped edge).

4. Pipe-in the centre of each poinsettia, as shown (No. 1). Leave to dry for 24 hours.

MAKING THE HOLLY LEAVES

2. Outline and flood-in each holly leaf on waxed paper (using template as a guide) (No. 1). Leave to dry in various positions for 24 hours. 30 leaves required. Paint veins with edible food colouring.

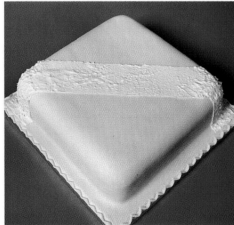

DECORATING THE CAKE

5. Stipple the part of the cake-top and corners shown. Leave to dry for 2 hours.

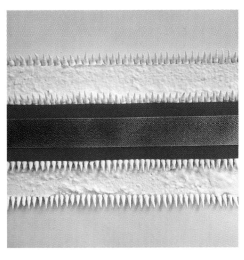

6. Fix a wide and a narrow ribbon to the cake-top. Pipe icicles on the ribbon edge, where shown (No. 1). Then pipe icicles against the stippled edge (No. 1).

9. Fix holly leaves to each piped design.

7. Pipe curved lines on the cake-top corners as shown (No. 2).

10. Pipe berries at the base of each leaf, as shown (No. 1).

8. Fix 3 poinsettias to each piped design.

11. Pipe curved lines around cake-base (No. 2). Then decorate with poinsettias, leaves and berries.

WORK NOTES

12. Fix ribbon loops, bells, holly leaves and berries to the cake-top centre.

13. Fix ribbon loops, bells and artificial flowers to the stippled cake-base corners.

COST SUMMARY

DATE _____ NAME _____ BOOK _____

PAGE _____ SIZE _____ SHAPE _____

CAKE _____ COVERING _____ COATING _____

A PRODUCTS	Used	Cost	B TIME TAKEN	Minutes
_____	_____	_____	_____	_____
_____	_____	_____	_____	_____
_____	_____	_____	_____	_____
_____	_____	_____	_____	_____
_____	_____	_____	_____	_____
_____	_____	_____	_____	_____
_____	_____	_____	_____	_____
_____	_____	_____	_____	_____
_____	_____	_____	_____	_____
_____	_____	_____	_____	_____
_____	_____	_____	Total	_____

Charge per minute × p

Total _____

LABOUR CHARGE Subtotal **B** = £ _____

Subtotals **A** + **B** = TOTAL COST = £ _____

OVERHEAD COSTS = £ _____

PROFIT COSTS = £ _____

GRAND TOTAL = £ _____

Subtotal: **A** = £ _____

NOTE: Please refer to the information on pages 5–10 before attempting to complete this COST SHEET. A 'MASTER' Cost Sheet can be found on page 116.

Christmas

CHRISTMAS'S CAKE PROFILE OCCASION – CHRISTMAS				
CAKE	– FRUIT CAKE			PAGE 16
SHAPE	– ROUND	23cm	9in	
BOARD	– ROUND	30.5cm	12in	
COVERING	– ALMOND PASTE	905g	2lb	PAGE 17
COATING	– ROYAL ICING	570g	1lb 4oz	PAGE 19
PIPING	– ROYAL ICING	340g	12oz	PAGE 19
DECORATION	– SUGARPASTE	170g	6oz	PAGE 17

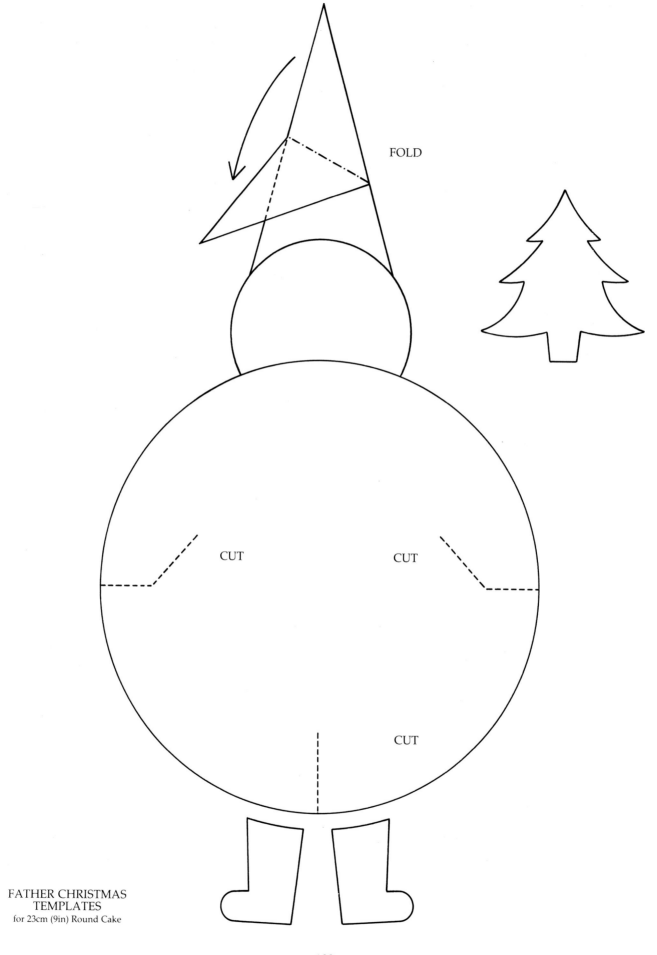

FOLD

CUT   CUT

CUT

FATHER CHRISTMAS
TEMPLATES
for 23cm (9in) Round Cake

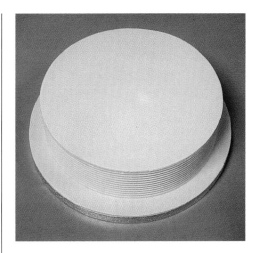

1. Picture showing the coated cake (with combed side) on its coated board.

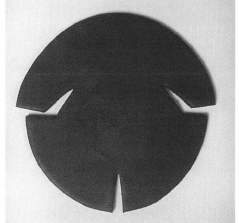

MAKING FATHER CHRISTMAS
2. Roll out, cut, shape and fix a sugarpaste disc to the cake-top, using the template as a guide.

3. Roll out, cut and fix the further sugarpaste shapes shown, using the template as a guide.

4. Decorate the Father Christmas head with sugarpaste and piped royal icing.

5. Decorate Father Christmas with sugarpaste and piped royal icing (No. 42).

MAKING CHRISTMAS TREES
6. Roll out, cut and fix sugarpaste trees to the cake-side, using the template as a guide. Pipe 'snow' on tree-tops and around the cake-base.

WORK NOTES

MAKING FATHER
CHRISTMAS
STEPS 2–5

TIME

STARTED   ———————

FINISHED   ———————

TIME TAKEN   ———————

MAKING CHRISTMAS
TREES
STEP 6

TIME

STARTED   ———————

FINISHED   ———————

TIME TAKEN   ———————

WORK NOTES

DECORATING THE CAKE
STEPS 7–8

TIME

STARTED _____

FINISHED _____

TIME TAKEN _____

DECORATING THE CAKE
7. Roll out, cut and fix a Father Christmas sack. Decorate with ribbon and piped snow.

8. Pipe message of choice on cake-top (No. 1). Then pipe shells and scrolls around cake-top edge (No. 43). Fix ribbon around cake-board edge.

COST SUMMARY

DATE _____ NAME _____ BOOK _____
PAGE _____ SIZE _____ SHAPE _____
CAKE _____ COVERING _____ COATING _____

A PRODUCTS	Used	Cost
_____	_____	_____
_____	_____	_____
_____	_____	_____
_____	_____	_____
_____	_____	_____
_____	_____	_____
_____	_____	_____
_____	_____	_____
_____	_____	_____
_____	_____	_____
_____	_____	_____
_____	_____	_____
_____	_____	_____
_____	_____	_____
_____	_____	_____
_____	_____	_____
_____	_____	_____
_____	_____	_____
_____	_____	_____
	Subtotal: **A** = £ _____	

B TIME TAKEN	Minutes
_____	_____
_____	_____
_____	_____
_____	_____
_____	_____
_____	_____
_____	_____
_____	_____
_____	_____
Total	_____
Charge per minute	× p
Total	_____
LABOUR CHARGE	Subtotal **B** = £ _____

Subtotals **A** + **B** = TOTAL COST = £ _____
OVERHEAD COSTS = £ _____
PROFIT COSTS = £ _____
GRAND TOTAL = £ _____

NOTE: Please refer to the information on pages 5–10 before attempting to complete this COST SHEET. A 'MASTER' Cost Sheet can be found on page 116.

Gloria

GLORIA'S CAKE PROFILE
OCCASION – NEW YEAR

CAKE	– FRUIT CAKE			PAGE 16
SHAPE	– SQUARE	20.5cm	8in	
BOARD	– ROUND	35.5cm	14in	
COVERING	– ALMOND PASTE	680g	1lb 8oz	PAGE 17
COATING	– ROYAL ICING	680g	1lb 8oz	PAGE 19
PIPING	– ROYAL ICING	225g	8oz	PAGE 19

WORK NOTES

DECORATING THE CAKE
STEPS 3–8

TIME

STARTED   ———————

FINISHED   ———————

TIME TAKEN   ———————

CAKE BOARD RUNOUT
STEP 2

TIME

STARTED   ———————

FINISHED   ———————

TIME TAKEN   ———————

1. Picture showing an open booked shaped cake (with combed sides – to give book pages effect) on its board.

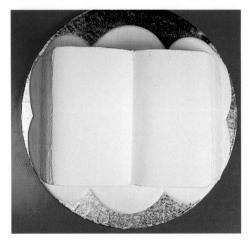

CAKE-BOARD RUNOUT
2. Outline (No. 2) and flood-in a scalloped runout border on cake-board. Leave to dry for 24 hours.

DECORATING THE CAKE
3. Pipe shells around cake-base (No. 43).

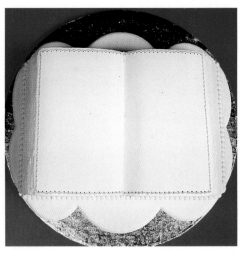

4. Pipe decorative lines and dots around cake-top edge, as shown (No. 1).

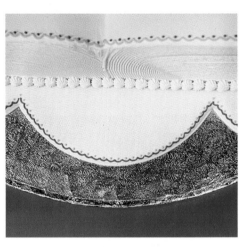

5. Pipe scalloped lines and dots on the cake-board runout, as shown (No. 1).

6. Pipe inscription of choice on left-hand side of cake-top and decorate, as shown (No. 1).

7. Pipe inscription of choice on right-hand side of cake-top and decorate, as shown (No. 1).

8. Fix ribbon to cake-top centre to form bookmark. Pipe the lines as shown (No. 1), then fix decorations of choice.

COST SUMMARY

DATE _____ NAME _____ BOOK _____
PAGE _____ SIZE _____ SHAPE _____
CAKE _____ COVERING _____ COATING _____

A PRODUCTS	Used	Cost
_____	_____	_____
_____	_____	_____
_____	_____	_____
_____	_____	_____
_____	_____	_____
_____	_____	_____
_____	_____	_____
_____	_____	_____
_____	_____	_____
_____	_____	_____
_____	_____	_____
_____	_____	_____
_____	_____	_____
_____	_____	_____
_____	_____	_____
_____	_____	_____
		Subtotal: **A** = £ _____

B TIME TAKEN Minutes

Total _____
Charge per minute × p
Total _____
LABOUR CHARGE Subtotal **B** = £ _____

Subtotals **A** + **B** = TOTAL COST = £ _____
OVERHEAD COSTS = £ _____
PROFIT COSTS = £ _____
GRAND TOTAL = £ _____

NOTE: Please refer to the information on pages 5–10 before attempting to complete this COST SHEET.
A 'MASTER' Cost Sheet can be found on page 116.

ALMOND PASTE COST SHEET

DATE MADE _____

A INGREDIENTS	Weight	Cost
_____	_____	_____
_____	_____	_____
_____	_____	_____
_____	_____	_____
_____	_____	_____
_____	_____	_____
_____	_____	_____
_____	_____	_____
	Subtotal **A** = £ _____	

B TIME TAKEN	Minutes
Making _____	_____
_____	_____
Total	_____
Charge per minute	× p
Total	_____
LABOUR CHARGE	Subtotal **B** = £ _____

Subtotals **A** + **B** = **TOTAL COST** = £ _____

TOTAL WEIGHT _____

ROYAL ICING COST SHEET

DATE MADE _____

A INGREDIENTS	Weight	Cost
_____	_____	_____
_____	_____	_____
_____	_____	_____
_____	_____	_____
_____	_____	_____
_____	_____	_____
_____	_____	_____
	Subtotal **A** = £ _____	

B TIME TAKEN	Minutes
Making _____	_____
_____	_____
Total	_____
Charge per minute	× p
Total	_____
LABOUR CHARGE	Subtotal **B** = £ _____

Subtotals **A** + **B** = **TOTAL COST** = £ _____

TOTAL WEIGHT (approx) _____

BUTTERCREAM COST SHEET

DATE MADE _____

A INGREDIENTS	Weight	Cost
_____	_____	_____
_____	_____	_____
_____	_____	_____
_____	_____	_____
_____	_____	_____
_____	_____	_____
_____	_____	_____
	Subtotal **A** = £ _____	

B TIME TAKEN	Minutes
Making _____	_____
_____	_____
Total	_____
Charge per minute	× p
Total	_____
LABOUR CHARGE	Subtotal **B** = £ _____

Subtotals **A** + **B** = **TOTAL COST** = £ _____

TOTAL WEIGHT _____

SUGAR PASTE COST SHEET

DATE MADE _____

A INGREDIENTS	Weight	Cost
_____	_____	_____
_____	_____	_____
_____	_____	_____
_____	_____	_____
_____	_____	_____
_____	_____	_____
_____	_____	_____
	Subtotal **A** = £ _____	

B TIME TAKEN	Minutes
Making _____	_____
_____	_____
Total	_____
Charge per minute	× p
Total	_____
LABOUR CHARGE	Subtotal **B** = £ _____

Subtotals **A** + **B** = **TOTAL COST** = £ _____

TOTAL WEIGHT (approx) _____

FLOWER PASTE COST SHEET

DATE MADE _____

A INGREDIENTS	Weight	Cost
_____	_____	_____
_____	_____	_____
_____	_____	_____
_____	_____	_____
_____	_____	_____
_____	_____	_____
_____	_____	_____
	Subtotal **A** = £ _____

B TIME TAKEN	Minutes
_____	_____
Making _____	_____
_____	_____
Total	_____
Charge per Minute	× p
Total	_____
LABOUR CHARGE	Subtotal **B** = £ _____

Subtotals **A** + **B** = **TOTAL COST** = £ _____

TOTAL WEIGHT _____

DATE MADE _____

A INGREDIENTS	Weight	Cost
_____	_____	_____
_____	_____	_____
_____	_____	_____
_____	_____	_____
_____	_____	_____
_____	_____	_____
_____	_____	_____
	Subtotal **A** = £ _____

B TIME TAKEN	Minutes
_____	_____
Making _____	_____
_____	_____
Total	_____
Charge per Minute	× p
Total	_____
LABOUR CHARGE	Subtotal **B** = £ _____

Subtotals **A** + **B** = **TOTAL COST** = £ _____

TOTAL WEIGHT _____

CAKE COST SHEET

CAKE _____ NAME _____ BOOK _____ PAGE _____

DATE MADE _____ SIZE _____ SHAPE _____

A INGREDIENTS	Weight	Cost
_____	_____	_____
_____	_____	_____
_____	_____	_____
_____	_____	_____
_____	_____	_____
_____	_____	_____
_____	_____	_____
_____	_____	_____
_____	_____	_____
_____	_____	_____
_____	_____	_____
_____	_____	_____
_____	_____	_____
_____	_____	_____
	Subtotal **A** = £ _____

C PRODUCTS	Used	Cost
_____	_____	_____
_____	_____	_____
_____	_____	_____
_____	_____	_____
	Subtotal **C** = £ _____

D TIME TAKEN	Minutes
_____	_____
Weighing	_____
Preparing Tin	_____
Making The Cake	_____
_____	_____
_____	_____
Total	_____
Charge per minute	× p
Total	_____
LABOUR CHARGE	Subtotal **D** = £ _____

B HEAT

10% of ingredients cost   Subtotal **B** = £ _____

Subtotals **A** + **B** + **C** + **D** =

TOTAL COST = £ _____

COATED CAKE COST SHEET

DATE _____ NAME _____ BOOK _____
PAGE _____ SIZE _____ SHAPE _____
CAKE _____ COVERING _____ COATING _____

A PRODUCTS	Used	Cost
_____	_____	_____
_____	_____	_____
_____	_____	_____
_____	_____	_____
_____	_____	_____
_____	_____	_____
_____	_____	_____
_____	_____	_____
_____	_____	_____
_____	_____	_____
_____	_____	_____
_____	_____	_____
_____	_____	_____
_____	_____	_____
	Subtotal **A** = £ _____	

B TIME TAKEN	Minutes
_____	_____
_____	_____
_____	_____
_____	_____
_____	_____
_____	_____
_____	_____
_____	_____
Total	_____
Charge per minute	× p
Total	_____
LABOUR CHARGE	Subtotal **B** = £ _____

Subtotals **A** + **B** = **TOTAL COST** = £ _____

COST SUMMARY

DATE _____ NAME _____ BOOK _____
PAGE _____ SIZE _____ SHAPE _____
CAKE _____ COVERING _____ COATING _____

A PRODUCTS	Used	Cost
_____	_____	_____
_____	_____	_____
_____	_____	_____
_____	_____	_____
_____	_____	_____
_____	_____	_____
_____	_____	_____
_____	_____	_____
_____	_____	_____
_____	_____	_____
_____	_____	_____
_____	_____	_____
_____	_____	_____
_____	_____	_____
_____	_____	_____
_____	_____	_____
	Subtotal: **A** = £ _____	

B TIME TAKEN	Minutes
_____	_____
_____	_____
_____	_____
_____	_____
_____	_____
_____	_____
_____	_____
_____	_____
_____	_____
Total	_____
Charge per minute	× p
Total	_____
LABOUR CHARGE	Subtotal **B** = £ _____

Subtotals **A** + **B** = TOTAL COST = £ _____
OVERHEAD COSTS = £ _____
PROFIT COSTS = £ _____
GRAND TOTAL = £ _____

IN ACCOUNT WITH
Mrs J. Smith. 15, Jasmine Road, Hometown, Parrish. _____ TEL ___ 519322 ___

CUSTOMER'S NAME ___ **Mrs S. Johnson** _____ DATE ___ **11th April (Year)** ___
CUSTOMER'S ADDRESS ___ **203, Fiveways, Hometown, Parrish.** ___

_____ TEL ___ 512397 ___

ORDER FORM

DATE OF CELEBRATION ___ **4th May** ___ FOR DELIVERY/COLLECTION ON ___ **3rd May** ___
DELIVER TO ___ **Shamrock Hotel, High Street, Hometown, Parrish.** ___

NAME OF CAKE DESIGN ___ **Wayne** ___ BOOK ___ **M.C.F.M.** ___ PAGES ___ **81–84** ___
SIZE ___ **20.5cm (8in)** ___ SHAPE ___ **Square** ___ COLOUR ___ **Blue** ___
INSCRIPTION ___ **Happy 18th Birthday James** ___

SPECIAL INSTRUCTIONS		COST
18 candles and holders	Cake	18.40
Deliver before 11 a.m.	Extra Decorations	.90
	Pillars	
	Top Ornament	
	Box(s)	.60
	Delivery	1.80
	Other	
	TOTAL PRICE	21.70
	Less Deposit Paid	11.00
	BALANCE TO PAY: £	10.70

Customer's Signature _____

Date ___ **11th April (YEAR)** ___

Top Copy – With Cake
2nd Copy – Customer
3rd Copy – For Records

ORDER FORM GUIDE

ALTHOUGH THE 'ORDER FORM' IS MAINLY SELF-EXPLANATORY, THE FOLLOWING NOTES MAY PROVE HELPFUL.

Always enter the cost of the completed cake – unless alterations are mutually agreed at the time of ordering. Such alterations should be clearly noted under 'SPECIAL INSTRUCTIONS' and costed at the time of order. Likewise, additional decorations, such as sugar swans, doves and flowers, must be costed and added to the Order Form, as well as any cake pillars and top ornament used.

Cake boxes used for collecting/delivering the cake(s) should be charged.

When appropriate, a 'delivery charge' at, say, the local taxi rate, is a proper charge.

Ensure the 'CAKE' ENTRY includes all ingredients, products and work from the 'COST SUMMARY'. Then add, as appropriate, the items listed on the Order Form.

ALWAYS receive a deposit (say 50%) of the total cost AT THE TIME OF RECEIVING THE ORDER. The balance to be collected prior to or at the time of collection/delivery.

Index/Glossary

MARY FORD TITLES

101 Cake Designs
ISBN: 0 946429 55 3   320 pages
The original Mary Ford cake artistry text book. A classic in its field, over 200,000 copies sold.

Cake Making and Decorating
ISBN: 0 946429 41 3   96 pages
Mary Ford divulges all the skills and techniques cake decorators need to make and decorate a variety of cakes in every medium.

Jams, Chutneys and Pickles
ISBN: 0 946429 48 0   96 pages
Over 70 of Mary Ford's favourite recipes for delicious jams, jellies, pickles and chutneys with hints and tips for perfect results.

Kid's Cakes
ISBN: 0 946429 53 7   96 pages
33 exciting new Mary Ford designs and templates for children's cakes in a wide range of mediums.

Children's Birthday Cakes
ISBN: 0 946429 46 4   112 pages
The book to have next to you in the kitchen! Over forty new cake ideas for children's cakes with an introduction on cake making and baking to ensure the cake is both delicious as well as admired.

Party Cakes
ISBN: 0 946429 13 8   120 pages
36 superb party time sponge cake designs and templates for tots to teenagers. An invaluable prop for the party cake decorator.

Quick and Easy Cakes
ISBN: 0 946429 42 1   208 pages
The book for the busy mum. 99 new ideas for party and special occasion cakes.

Decorative Sugar Flowers for Cakes
ISBN: 1 85479 405 1   120 pages
33 of the highest quality handcrafted sugar flowers with cutter shapes, background information and appropriate uses.

Cake Recipes
ISBN: 0 946429 43 X   96 pages
Contains 60 of Mary's favourite cake recipes ranging from fruit cake to cinnamon crumble cake.

One Hundred Easy Cake Designs
ISBN: 1 85479 420 5   208 pages
Mary Ford has originated 100 cakes all of which have been selected for ease and speed of making. The ideal book for the busy parent or friend looking for inspiration for a special occasion cake.

Wedding Cakes
ISBN: 0 946429 39 1   96 pages
For most cake decorators, the wedding cake is the most complicated item they will produce. This book gives a full step-by-step description of the techniques required and includes over 20 new cake designs.

Home Baking with Chocolate
ISBN: 0 946429 37 5   96 pages
Over 60 tried and tested recipes for cakes, gateaux, biscuits, confectionery and desserts. The ideal book for busy mothers.

Making Cakes for Money
ISBN: 1 85479 421 3   120 pages
The complete guide to making and costing cakes for sale at stalls or to friends. Invaluable advice on costing ingredients and time accurately.

Biscuit Recipes
ISBN: 0 946429 50 2   96 pages
Nearly 80 home-bake sweet and savoury biscuit and tray bake recipes chosen for variety and ease of making.

The New Book of Cake Decorating
ISBN: 1 85479 407 8   224 pages
The most comprehensive title in the Mary Ford list. It includes over 100 new cake designs and full descriptions of all the latest techniques.

A to Z of Cake Decorating
ISBN: 0 946429 52 9   208 pages
A guide to cake decorating, detailing traditional skills and the latest techniques. Over 70 new designs.

BOOKS BY MAIL ORDER

Mary Ford operates a mail order service in the U.K. for all her step-by-step titles. If you write to Mary at the address below she will provide you with a price list and details. In addition, all names on the list receive information on new books and special offers.

Write to: Mary Ford,
30 Duncliff Road,
Southbourne, Bournemouth,
Dorset. BH6 4LJ. England.